This Is China!

A Guidebook for Teachers, Backpackers and Other Lunatics

Megan Eaves

First edition printed 2009.
Copyright © 2009 by Megan Eaves
All rights reserved.

No part of this book may be reproduced, printed, copied or retransmitted in any form, digital or otherwise, without prior consent of the publisher.

ISBN No. 978-0-557-08118-9

Printed, bound and distributed through Lulu.com.
Printed in the U.S.A.

For more information, visit:
http://www.meganeaves.com

ACKNOWLEDGEMENTS

I must first thank Professor Zhu Jian for fostering my interest in Chinese and providing me with my earliest chances to visit China. Inspiration for this book came from an original trip preparation manual that I designed for the American Chinese Civic Exchange with the help of Todd Bernardy, Cameron Stark and Perry Muller. I also owe thanks to all of my friends, and former and current colleagues in China, especially Anastasia Searfoss and Claudia Schagerl, with whom I shared many a bottle of Tibetan wine while writing this book. Thanks to David Ding and Zhu Feiteng for placing me in great schools, and to Kenneth Christof for his lifelong friendship and the amazing time we spent in Shanghai together.

Special thanks to my parents, who have always fostered my independence and told me to travel, and to my grandmother who would have loved to see this book in print.

Most importantly, to Bill, my partner in crime and the love of my life, thank you for your constant encouragement, unending belief in me and for wanting a China adventure of your own.

For laowai everywhere.

Contents

Introduction	**1**
Chapter 1 - The Compulsory Stuff	**3**
Fact Files	5
Social Stuff: TIC!	8
Chapter 2 - Before You Go	**19**
Finding a Job	19
Getting Out	24
Packing	27
Chapter 3 - Arrival & Daily Life	**32**
Culture Shock	32
Logistics	33
Daily Living	38
Chapter 4 - On Being an FT	**45**
What to Expect	46
Teaching Game Plan	47
Exams & Grading	52
Recommendations & Materials	54
Resources	61
Chapter 5 - The Official Stuff	**63**
Signing Your Contract	63
In the Classroom	66
Strange Occurrences	70
Outside Tutoring	71
Chapter 6 - Food, Dining & Going Out	**73**
Chinese Food Basics	73
Dining Culture & The Banquet	76
Eating the Unusual	79
In a Restaurant	81
In the Kitchen	84
Going to the Market	85
Specialties	87

Chapter 7 - Cheap Thrills — 93
Western bars & pubs — 93
Chinese bars & discos — 94
Karaoke (KTV) — 94

Chapter 8 - Laowai Health — 97
Health Exam — 97
Common Ailments — 98
Dentists — 101
Sexual Health — 102

Chapter 9 - Becoming a Travel Junkie — 105
Public Transport — 106
Where to Stay — 113
Public Holidays — 115
Sightseeing — 119
Top 10 Must-Visit Places — 120
Top 10 Super Cool, Road-Less-Traveled Ideas — 123
Travel Tips & Tricks — 124

Chapter 10 - Laowai Dictionary — 129
On pinyin — 130
On grammar & tones — 132
Basic Necessities — 134
Keys to the Middle Kingdom — 144

Introduction
For the *Laowai*...

Anyone that has spent even a short amount of time in China can instantly recognize the term "lǎowài" [老外]. *Laowai* is Chinese slang for "foreign person," literally translated as "old foreigner." Most Chinese use this term more endearingly than rudely, but any Westerner that has spent even a short time in China has, invariably, heard the "Laowai!" catcalls of curious or mischievous streetside onlookers. Those of us who have survived life in China without jumping the next plane home have learned to embrace our *laowai'ism*, knowing, no matter how good our Chinese gets, if we dye our hair black, or wear boots over our jeans come winter, we will always, *always* be *laowai*.

This book is for us. Old hats and new brethren alike, we all face the same dilemmas, problems, and utter humiliations. That said, don't be scared. If you are considering a visit or move to China, this book is meant to help you. Sure, moving to China isn't an easy experience. People will probably think you are crazy. Hell, at some times, *you* will probably think you are crazy – and you might just be. Even still, this book isn't meant to frighten you off, it's meant to help and encourage you. One thing you probably already know is that this is going to be challenging. That's probably why you picked the book up in the first place. But, for all the difficult times ahead, there will be more fulfillment, peace, and excitement than you can imagine. If you're wavering, just take the plunge and go for it. It'll be worth it.

So, let this be a guide, a manual, a diary, a friend on those solo Tibetan wine nights, a pillow on a hard seat train, a writing tablet when you're giving autographs, reading material for the 20-minute silence between when you ask your students a question and the first hand that tentatively rises, a menu in the times when you can't muster the strength to just point and hope for the best. And most importantly, let this book be a source of help on the days you think you just won't make it another hour and a source of amusement on the days when life is so beautiful you can't remember existence at home.

TIC! This Is China...

The expression "This Is China" did not originate from one single person. It is not a catch phrase claimed by one individual who, in a moment of genius, staked the rights to the words. No, "This Is China" is simply the catch-all retort that every laowai uses when he or she has no other explanation to offer for the strange incidents that inevitably happen in this country.

Most often, the phrase is uttered to oneself in a flash of sheer frustration or complete confusion about *why* a particular event is occurring. Let me assure you of one thing: This will, without a doubt, become the most useful phrase in your Chinese life. You will have schedule changes with no notice. There will be chickens on your hard seat from Shanghai to Hangzhou. You will inexplicably be moved from teaching Senior 3 to teaching First Year with four minutes' notice. Your illegal copy of "Pirates of the Caribbean" will turn out to be the Jack Palance version of "Treasure Island". It is during times such as those, when you are stranded on a bus that has randomly stopped on the side of the road for no apparent reason in the 30-degree heat for several hours, that no other phrase will aptly capture the sheer perplexity of it all. You can join the club to which we've all succumbed and simply say, *Well, what can you do?*

This is China!

Chapter 1
The Compulsory Stuff

China is the most populous nation on earth with almost a billion and a half people now living there, and that is only one of several reasons for the growing foreign interest in the Middle Kingdom. Every year, more Westerners flock to China on business trips, leisure outings and teaching stints than any other country in Asia. And if you looked at this book with even a passing glance, then you have some interest in the country, too.

It's no secret that the Chinese government is a communist system. Foreign media love to splash that fact about as they market China as the next big doom and, while they might be right, there is much more to China than just inflated oil use and the infamous million man army.

Chinese people are often keen to remind foreigners about their country's long history – 5,000 years! Chinese history is divided into smaller eras, known as dynasties, named for the ruling clans during those periods. It is commonly accepted that China was first united under the Emperor Qin Shi Huang in the year 221 B.C., marking the Qin Dynasty and the start of the Imperial period. Succeeding dynasties assumed command as ruling clans gained control or overran one another and placed their own emperors in power.

The Republic of China was formed in 1912, after revolutionaries overthrew the Qing Dynasty emperor. This marked the beginning of an unstable period where warlords ruled over lower classes and local clans constantly battled for power. The People's Republic of China was instituted until 1949 by Mao Zedong and is the communist system still in place today. This change took place after nearly 30 years of internal and foreign conflicts, including World War II and the Japanese occupation of China.

Mao was also responsible for the Great Proletarian Cultural Revolution (1966-1975), a chaotic and violent campaign to rid China of its liberal bourgeoisie elements and revert to a plebeian, agricultural society. Mao wanted to abolish what he termed the 'Four Olds': old customs, culture, habits and ideas. It was during this Cultural Revolution that many forms of art, music, architecture, painting, and calligraphy were lost and religion was abolished. Additionally, Mao called for a simplification of society, including the development of Simplified Written Chinese, where characters were pared down from the older, more intricate forms to facilitate quick writing.

Fact Files

China's borders span to nearly 9.6 million sq. km., roughly the size of the United States, making it one of the largest countries on earth in terms of landmass. The Red Giant is home to mountains and rivers, lakes and tea fields, deserts and grasslands. It is undoubtedly one of the most diverse and beautiful countries in the world.

Language

Hundreds of different nationalities and languages exist in China, the largest of those being the Han culture and language (often referred to as Mandarin). Anyone who has spent even a minimal amount of time trying to hone their *pǔtōnghuà* (普通话 'common speech'), a.k.a. Standard Mandarin Chinese, knows that the breadth of 'local dialects' within China can be both intimidating and maddening.

One thing to consider about Standard Mandarin is that it is actually a *contrived* language based off of the northern Beijing dialects. Unlike Standard English, which developed out of a natural progression from the way scholars and intellects spoke and what they valued in their language, Putonghua was actually *created* by the government during the Cultural Revolution in an effort to build a more unified nation-state. This ends up being very important in China, which has 56 *recognized* minority groups with native languages, not to mention all of the dialects of Chinese that also exist. In almost every province, region, county, and sometimes even city, you will hear variations of Chinese being spoken, some more intelligible than others. Some of these dialects are arguably not even dialects at all, as they are so different that even a Chinese outsider cannot understand a significant percentage of what is being said.

While all of these facts and stats may be a linguist's dream, they are not so important for the average China-beginner, except to say that, when you're trying out your Chinese listening and speaking skills for the first time, don't feel bad if you don't understand what's going on. It's entirely possible that a native Chinese speaker might not know either. Just go with the flow. After some time in your respective area, you will begin to hear the difference between the infamous 'local language' and Putonghua. Luckily for us, Putonghua is taught in school, so most Chinese are able to get by with it. At least, that's what we tell ourselves to avoid utter and total humiliation.

Weather

Well, that all depends on where in China you are. There are, however, two rules that apply almost everywhere in China: summer is stiflingly hot and winter is numbingly cold. Expect to sweat profusely from May to October, and come prepared with clothing that breathes. Likewise, come ready to shiver from November to April. Chinese buildings aren't well insulated. Scratch that, they aren't insulated at all. So, unless you live in one of the southern provinces like Guangdong, you probably be bundled during winter, and you may even pick up that nightly laowai habit of drinking a glass of wine to keep the blood from freezing completely over. The monsoon season occurs in late summer, so also expect rain and, if you're in a coastal area, typhoons.

Pollution

Environmental awareness is purportedly on the rise in China, but it's difficult to spot. In terms of pollution, China is still a developing nation. Read: It's dirty. The air is heavily polluted, especially in large cities like Shanghai and Beijing. Smog density is intensified by the heat and humidity in the summer, and rains do little to bring the haze down. You may not see much blue sky during your time in China and you'll learn to revel in those fleeting sunny days when the sky is blue, and you can ride your bicycle all afternoon to enjoy it.

Time difference

China operates on Beijing Standard Time, which is London +8, New York +13, Los Angeles +16. China has not instituted a daylight savings system, so the time differences vary throughout the year, when half the world *is* on daylight savings (at that time, Beijing Time is London +7). Also, the Beijing government feels that the entire country is just fine and dandy to operate on one time zone. Therefore, all 2000 miles of Chinese landmass are always on the same time. This means that, in the west of China, the sun sets very late during summer. It's also notable that those areas sometimes operate on unofficial 'local time zones'.

Money

Chinese currency is called the Renminbi (人民币 'people's money'), usually abbreviated as RMB. The symbol for RMB is ¥ and the units are called *yuán*, (slang is *kuài* which actually means 'piece') and *jiǎo*. 1 yuan = 10 jiao. Jiao are like dimes, and yuan are like dollars. These come in both bills and coins, although the jiao bills are currently on the way out. There were formerly 1-cent denominations called *fēn*, but they have now become obsolete.

Water

Tap water in China is not drinking-quality, but bottled water is everywhere. Most places, including classrooms in many areas, have purified water spouts, and the locals usually boil water in an electric kettle for drinking and cooking. You can also purchase large purified water dispensers to use in your home. Remember that cold/ice water is not a norm in China, so expect to drink lukewarm or boiled water! A hint: dropping one or two tea pods in your bottle can make the water tastier!

Běi 北 and Nán 南 - North vs. South

Thanks to a history of social collectivism combined with the current communist system, Chinese culture tends to be fairly homogeneous. However, two large cultural regions do exist in China (along with handfuls of other, smaller ones). Geographically, these are north and south. Most Chinese people recognize these regions, and there are stigmas between each group. The dividing line is around the Yangtze River (长江 cháng jiāng) which flows from the western alpine regions, cutting across the mid-section of China, and eventually pouring out to the East China Sea north of Shanghai. This line is somewhat comparable to the north/south divide in the United States. Northerners might view Southerners as unrefined, rural bumpkins. Southerners sometimes complain that Northerners are distant, cold and caustic. These stereotypes are just that, and you will find that, generally, Chinese people are friendly, open, and welcoming.

The cultures of the regions do vary noticeably, though, as do the languages. Southerners use a surplus of words to convey politeness, while Northern language is a bit more direct and less flowery. In and around Beijing, you can hear the famous *er hua* dialects, or Beijing accents, which are marked by the excessive use of 'r' sounds and guttural noises. Culturally, each region has its own customs, traditions and foods, so you'll have a chance to explore your own region thoroughly. Traveling around China makes an interesting comparison of the various cultural groups.

Social Stuff: TIC!

"Culture shock can't be measured in volts, but the jolt sent through most Westerners the first time they see and smell a Chinese toilet is roughly equivalent to sticking a fork in a socket." - letsgo.com

On being flexible...

The first time I came to China, it was for a one-month summer English and cultural exchange program. We were to teach Middle School students for three weeks in Nanjing and then spend one week touring in Beijing. As an appointed program assistant, I was expected to take care of some logistical details and program scheduling. When I arrived, I realized that my job was *actually* to take up the slack when there was a last-minute schedule change, or to perform on two minutes' notice, or to speak well in front of TV cameras with absolutely no preparation. Basically, it was to do the unexpected.

To survive any length of time in China means to be flexible. Whether you are living here, or just touring around for a couple of weeks, you will find you *must* be flexible. Life in another culture always means having to adapt, but the amount of adapting that a Westerner must do in China sometimes seems preposterous. I can, however, make this guarantee: if you don't learn to go with the flow, your life will be unbearable. Vague answers, lack of planning, short (aka NO) notice, constant change, scheduling conflicts, more vague answers, complete and total inability to get anything done, asking for something ten times before you get anywhere... The list could go on for a while, but this is a big part of being in China, and something you simply must get used to.

This aspect of Chinese life is really one of the most difficult things for Westerners, especially Americans, to adapt to. We rely on schedules and plans and often feel uncomfortable being in the dark. In Chinese culture, however, planning is not as salient and vague answers are the norm as a face-saving activity (see *Mianzi*).

These are the situations where TIC becomes a very useful phrase. Eventually, you will probably get frustrated to an angry degree. Getting angry with school officials or your Foreign Expert Officer probably won't help the situation, and it certainly won't do anything to speed them up. Things are going to take the time they take regardless of how you respond, so really, you are doing yourself a favor to be as relaxed as possible about the lack of planning and constant change.

Guanxi - 关系 gūanxi

Guanxi is the Chinese practice of relationships, wherein favors are exchanged between two parties to accomplish things and garner benefits with others. Guanxi is vital to the Chinese social structure, and average people practice it on a daily basis, sometimes even subconsciously. It can come in many forms and is difficult to define, but usually involves helping out friends, bringing gifts, complimenting or providing services – whatever one is capable of or particularly adept at may be called on in a guanxi situation.

In China, a collective society, values revolve around group participation and dedication to the community. Therefore, guanxi is essentially obligatory to function within society. This kind of, "You scratch my back, I'll scratch yours" mentality is oftentimes distasteful to Westerners because it seems like bribery. In China, however, doing favors is very positive, and really, nothing gets done otherwise.

You may notice your Chinese colleagues or school officials asking you to do favors for them – or rather, presenting you with tasks outside your official, contractual duties and simply expecting you to perform them. This is guanxi at work. While you may feel hesitant to do them, you can certainly reap the benefits of these tasks, as your colleagues will, no doubt, be there to help you out at a later time. If you plan to succeed in China or hope to be accepted as a participant in Chinese society, it will aid you to cooperate in guanxi actions. Bring gifts to others' homes, offer small tokens or compliments to people when they weren't asked for, and make yourself available for extracurricular tasks. By creating these connections, you'll later be able to draw from a large pool of potential helpers when sticky situations arise. (Though it should be noted that schools sometimes take advantage of foreign teachers, asking them to work unpaid days or during holidays, which I do not condone).

One place where Westerners often mistakenly try to garner guanxi is within commerce. Guanxi is not the way to make life easier when shopping or reducing the price of a meal. Within the marketplace, guanxi is rather useless, especially if you are a laowai. Being extra-nice to a rude shopkeeper isn't going to make her like you more, nor is it going to reduce the price of that umbrella you're bargaining for. Save your guanxi for people that you'll be interacting with on personal, career and political levels. Remember: guanxi is about doing favors, not necessarily about being friendly to strangers.

Mianzi - 面子 miànzi

Miànzi, or *liǎn*, are concepts of 'face'. This idea is most familiar in the expression 'saving face'; that is to say, not being publicly disrespectful to others, or taking preventative actions to ensure that others aren't embarrassed. Though most cultures have some notion of face, it is essential in China. To distinguish between the two, *liǎn* is social confidence one's moral character, while *miànzi* is the social observation of one's prestige.

Group harmony is of absolute importance in collective societies such as China. People dislike direct confrontation, including expressing a clear 'no'. Oftentimes, your questions will be answered with "Maybe so," "It's possible", or "We'll see". These evasive and inaccurate statements are used to keep appearances pleasant by avoiding negative repercussions should plans change at a later time. So, vague, unclear answers are common in China. The upshot is that what Westerners would consider a lie is not necessarily immoral or bad, but simply a statement made to protect group harmony. 'Polite lies', or those 'little white' ones, are actually expected and can be easily interpreted by skillful Chinese communicators.

Ways of Losing Face
- exposed personal inadequacy
- failure to reach goals
- making what may be seen as an 'unnecessary' compromise
- being forced to give up a beloved object
- a personal insult
- a derogatory remark or slight of one's status
- a rejected proposal
- damaging a valued relationship

The important distinction here is that collective cultures want to repair or build relationships but individualist cultures (like North American and European ones) prefer to problem-solve and move on. Keep this in mind as you try to communicate (even in English) on a daily basis. Coming from an individualist culture and trying to communicate in a collective one is confusing and trying, even for experienced communication professionals. Learn to be aware of your communication styles and notice how they seem to differ from your Chinese counterparts. This will lead you to more effective role-playing within the social structure.

Modesty

If you read the analects of Confucius, you will find dozens of quotes about modesty and humility, and it's one of the ways that Confucianism still shows up strongly in Chinese culture today. Modesty is most often displayed as refusal to accept gifts, downplaying one's own talents or self-deprecating speech acts. For instance, a Chinese person will often reject a gift (even a small token) several times before finally accepting it. It is important to play along and insist that the recipient take the gift because, if you withdraw the offer too soon, the recipient may feel hurt or offended and might not understand why you retracted so quickly while they were only being polite.

The same goes for any gift or generous offer made to you. Initially, it is most polite to modestly refuse several times before finally accepting the offer. When being complimented, Chinese people will often look down, cover their mouths and tell you that you are incorrect or make another self-deprecating remark. This is most commonly observed when you tell someone they speak English well, where the response would be, "No, no. My English is so poor."

If you want to earn face and respect among Chinese people, engaging in this kind of modesty will get you a lot of points. It may feel strange at first; however, Chinese people are often very uncomfortable with the Western practice of simply saying "Thank you" when a compliment is received. In their eyes, it seems arrogant and they may perceive you to be very conceited.

Out in Public

Bathrooms – 厕所 cèsuǒ

The biggest complaint among new laowai is that no one warned them about Chinese toilets. Consider this your warning! Bathrooms in China are one of the more frightening things you'll ever encounter on this planet. They are smelly and dirty and generally pretty unpleasant. Toilets are usually of the 'squatter' variety, although your accommodation (apartment, hostel or hotel) should have a Western style 'seater' potty. However, if you venture into a public bathroom, all bets are off. Expect to find a squatter, sometimes accompanied by a chain pulley flush and on occasion, without a stall or door. It is advisable to carry tissues at all times (especially women, though, guys, you might want to pack some for those emergency cases, 'cause there will be some!). You can buy cute little packets that fit into your purse or pocket, and some even come in scented varieties. Also, you should note that the little basket filled with papers next to the toilet is for throwing used papers, not a dispenser for free papers. Toilets clog easily, so get used to tossing your used paper in the trash rather than flushing it, even at home.

A tip for the ladies on how to use the squatter: before entering the stall, roll your trousers up to your knees. Really hunker down. If you squat too high, you will experience unpleasant repercussions. Also, don't stand on the 'foot sliders' that are provided, stand on the floor outside the toilet rim. Hold your breath and go as quickly as possible. And don't roll your trousers down until you exit the stall!

Staring

These days, foreigners aren't uncommon in China. However, they aren't a dime a dozen, either. Even in larger cities, Chinese people are often still surprised to see laowai. Their surprise quickly turns to consternation and that results in staring. In English, there is the saying, "Didn't your mother ever teach you not to stare?" No such thing exists in Chinese. It's simply not rude to stare. In fact, staring represents curiosity and, for Chinese people, curiosity equals good.

In a collective society like China, group rather than individual identity is promoted. Staring isn't the only result of this collective mindset – you'll find strangers are more eager to help one another and they take on personal conversations with ease. Likewise, once they get past the initial shock of seeing a laowai, Chinese people will often go out of their way to help you if you need it. Sure, it takes awhile to get used to the staring, but try smiling back. More often than not, this breaks the stare and initiates contact, and suddenly they remember you are a human being, not just a foreign face.

Public Hygiene

Okay, so China is not the cleanest place ever, in terms of pretty much everything. Rubbish is cast about with little regard for the consequences. Often, people simply burn their trash, adding to the imminent haze that covers most of the nation. Students tend to disregard any cleanliness rules that might exist in schools, and their elders certainly set no good example, as grown adults will simply throw plastic wrappers on the ground or roadside. Sadly, at the time of writing, very little environmental education was occurring in China, although environmental awareness is steadily rising. One of the best things you can do for yourself and your friends and acquaintances in China is to set a good example. Make a point to pick up your rubbish or go out of your way to find trash bins. Students and friends *will* notice this and hopefully follow your lead.

Another thing that you will inevitably see at some point is public urination/defecation, usually by small children or babies, although I've observed pretty much every age group doing this at one time or another. Babies are often publicly potty trained, meaning they are asked to go just about anywhere when the time comes. Babies also don't wear diapers, but rather strange little outfits with slits down the behind for easy access. It's at this point that we have to keep in mind, as China is developing and changing rapidly, so these cultural norms are also becoming different. In larger, more cosmopolitan cities, you'll probably see this kind of thing less than you do in smaller farming towns. Nonetheless, it happens and it's part of Chinese culture at the present. Do your best not to let it freak you out and, instead, try to get some good photos of it! A thousand points if you capture twin bottoms! It's all part of the experience!

Spitting

Along with the lack of mindfulness about public hygiene comes spitting. It's quite simply culturally okay to spit in public. This is something that takes many laowai a long time to get used to. Everywhere you go, you will hear people hocking and spitting – on the street, in restaurants, at home... literally, *everywhere*. It's possible that the amount of air pollution in China now contributes to generally poor lung capacities and/or grime in the respiration system. It's also possible that spitting has just always been done. Whatever the reason, it's simply a fact of life.

Tipping

Tipping is simply not done in China, which is actually true in many parts of the world. The reasons for this vary, but really, tipping is *quite* a Western thing, particularly in the United States, where servers don't earn minimum wage, so the tip becomes necessary to making livable money.

Conversely, in China, service jobs are paid as any other jobs, so servers don't need to rely on tips to earn their full wages. Additionally, in some cases, tipping can even represent an offense, in that servers simply expect to do their job and be paid for it. So, a tip comes across as condescending. Generally speaking, workers in China, whatever their occupations, take great pride in their jobs and usually have a good work ethic. Finally, as we've seen, China tends to be a collective society, but tipping is a monetary reward of individual achievement. With a tip, you are essentially saying, "*You* did a good job." Chinese people will shy away from this kind of individualized recognition and, instead, promote a feeling of group achievement. They prefer the idea of 'we' to the idea of 'me' or 'you'. Basically, unless you're in a very high-end Western hotel or restaurant and gratuity is included in the bill, just don't tip.

Gifts - 礼物 lǐwù

Gift-giving is a major tradition in China, and plays an important role in developing guanxi. If you're moving to China, you might want to prepare gifts for about 10-20 people: students, colleagues, and important officials you'll meet during your first few days and weeks. Don't spend more than $1-5 per gift, and make sure they do not say "Made in China!" Your gifts should reflect yourself and, traditionally, should be wrapped in red tissue paper. Suitable gifts might be small tokens from your hometown like pins or magnets, or anything that will remind the recipient of you. Obviously, giving items that cannot be found in China is ideal. Also, when visiting a friend or colleague's home, it's very polite to bring a gift. This practice also contributes to guanxi. In these cases, fruit or flowers make very nice gifts, or else some small, inexpensive decoration is appropriate.

Peddlers, Touts & Beggars

In larger cities, especially in tourist areas, peddlers abound. There will likely be a barrage of salesmen flogging Chinese flags, Mao watches, DVDs and a sundry of other items. These peddlers often heavily overcharge foreign tourists, who think they are getting a steal in comparison with Western prices. Never follow a peddler somewhere out of a main area or trust anyone that approaches you on the street offering a good deal.

When arriving in stations or at taxi stands, you will encounter touts. These are local drivers hoping you'll hire them to take you to your destination. Touts are useful *only* when you're in a real bind for transportation, but never take a tout as your first option. More often than not, there are nearby public transport options that are safer and cheaper than what touts will offer. Check for official ticket windows before bargaining with a tout.

The best way to deal with anyone who approaches you on the street (particularly in big cities or tourist areas) is to simply ignore them. Even saying, "No thank you" will usually just encourage them to follow you or continue bothering you. Don't be afraid to be brusque and just tell them to piss off!

Major Scams

In the larger Chinese cities, several scams occur that are geared to foreign tourists, especially those who look lost or naive. Usually, one or several sweet/innocent/friendly Chinese college students who undoubtedly speak excellent English will approach you. At first, it will seem as though they simply want to make conversation or practice their English, but beware!

Art Students

Several students strike up conversation with you in a public place. They claim to be from another area of China, just arrived to study art. They are very friendly and finally offer for you to take a look at some of their artwork, usually in an apartment or studio to which they offer to lead you. Once at the studio, you will be pressured into buying some of these pieces of artwork, which are usually very poor quality knock-offs of ancient Chinese style scroll paintings. These 'students' actually work for organizations that produce fake artwork to be sold in such a manner.

Tea House/Ceremony

Again, one or several twenty-somethings will approach you on the street and strike up random conversation. Eventually, they will somehow mention they are going to a tea ceremony, or offer to be your guide around the city. They will seem very friendly and helpful. They'll take you to a teahouse, where you will order and sample teas and eventually be presented the bill (if you don't offer to pay), which can range upwards of several hundreds (or in some cases, thousands) of yuan. These "friendly students" are actually family members or employees of the teahouses, which earn profits by scamming Westerners into buying inexpensive tea at ungodly prices.

Gesture and Touch

Chinese public touching rules are often really difficult to handle. In a country of more than a billion people, you're going to encounter serious crowds. Pushing, shoving and general mass touching are not unusual. Lining up (排队 páiduì) is not custom in China, so you'll learn quickly how to push and shove your way to the front if you ever want to get anything done, particularly getting on a bus, buying tickets, waiting at a restaurant, etc.

During introductions, Chinese will generally initiate a handshake, but may also bow slightly. A simple handshake is polite, but bear in mind that Chinese prefer to use a quick, limp hand instead of a firm shake. Try to avoid showing the soles of your shoes. Pointing with one index finger is very rude, so use an open hand instead. Also, when motioning for someone to come closer, the Chinese will put their hand out with the palm down and pull the fingers toward themselves (as opposed to the American way, which is to put the palm up and pull the pointer finger).

Traffic

Traffic in China is horrific. If rules of the road exist, no one abides by them. At least half the time, you find yourself wondering if drivers even bothered to get licenses (or if licenses are even required, at that). Roads are chaotic and, if lines happen to be painted, they are generally disregarded, as are stoplights and other traffic signs. Signaling is virtually unheard of. Anything you can possibly imagine occurring on the road does – driving the wrong way or reversing on a highway, hopping the curb, driving on the sidewalk, overtaking with oncoming traffic and more. Biking and even walking on the street can be dangerous. Two good rules of thumb for staying alive on Chinese roads: 1) Always look where you are going – walk/bike/stand defensively. 2) The bigger vehicle has the right of way and you are responsible for getting out of the way, lest you be run over.

All this chaos on the streets of China has led to a superabundance of honking, which is not considered rude. Chinese drivers tend to use their horns like turn signals to warn other drivers of their presence. This can be incredibly annoying and sometimes it's difficult to put away your Western sensibilities about politeness when a driver stares you in the eye and honks unrelentingly at you. Nonetheless, it's actually *more* polite to honk than not and could arguably be traced to social collectivism in that drivers are simply trying to take care of one another. Whatever the case may be, be prepared for the noisy harem on the streets, and arm yourself with earplugs or headphones on long bus rides when drivers tend to lay on the huge, ear-splitting air horns at every bend.

Chapter 2
Before You Go

Finding a Job

Perhaps the most dauntingly difficult part of going to teach in China is finding a job. While there are literally thousands of jobs for foreign teachers in Chinese schools each year, it can be troublesome to sort through websites, job advertisements, recruiters and schools. While much of the foreign teaching sector in China is fairly similar across the board, there are a few different types of situations on offer and even more ways to get yourself into trouble if you aren't careful.

You will generally need to hold at least a B.A. degree, with higher pay scales for those with postgraduate degrees. Some schools will hire foreigners with no degree certificate, but they are difficult to find and don't usually provide proper working conditions. You won't need to have an extensive ESL (English as a Second Language) certificate, such as the CELTA or TESOL, but it would be a good idea to take a short course or online TEFL (Teaching English as a Foreign Language) certification program to obtain basic information about how to teach English as a foreign language. As well, most Chinese provinces require some sort of teaching certification in order to supply the work permit and Foreign Expert certifications that must be issued for a Z working visa.

The first thing to decide is whereabouts you want to live. Does it have to be a large cosmopolitan city like Shanghai, a small mid-level Chinese city with fewer Western amenities, or do you prefer living in a very rural setting? The vast majority of Chinese teaching situations are on offer in mid-level Chinese towns, while the jobs in major cities like Shanghai are coveted and competitive. Chinese semesters begin in September and February/March, with the most jobs commencing in the autumn. You'll want to start job hunting up to a several months in advance, as that is how long it will take to secure the right job and make all the necessary visa and travel arrangements. The last thing you want to be doing is biting your fingernails waiting for last-minute paperwork to arrive and forking over wads of cash to get your visa rushed.

Types of Schools

There are two types of schools available in China: public and private. Public schools are far more trustworthy, as they are run under state guidelines and generally follow the correct legal standards, including being licensed to hire foreign teachers by the State Administration for Foreign Expert Affairs (SAFEA). The working schedule in public schools should be no more than 20 hours per week, full time, and public schools should provide free accommodation to teachers, as well as work permits and invitation letters to process the Z working visa for your arrival to China. Salaries for foreign teachers giving Oral English classes in public schools range from ¥3,000-8,000 per month, depending on location and whether or not the teacher has a postgraduate degree. Most public schools offer one month of winter vacation time (paid), one to two months of summer vacation time, plus all national bank holidays. Furthermore, many schools offer a free travel stipend to foreign teachers (generally between ¥1000-3000 per year) and pay part or all of the teacher's airfare to China.

Private schools range from large boarding schools that look and feel much like a public school (and generally offer the same salaries and working conditions as a public school), to small training centers that work mostly on evenings and weekends giving lessons to all age groups. Working in a private training school, you are bound to have far more hours (up to 40 hours) than at a public school (20 hours), might not be given free accommodation or airfare reimbursement, and might also be offered a higher salary (though you *will* work for it). Additionally, private schools may offer different/less holiday time than public schools, a lot of weekend and night work, or no two consecutive days off in a week. The other problem with private schools is that many are not legally licensed by SAFEA to hire foreign teachers. Thus, many will try to lure you into arriving in China on a tourist visa or teaching illegally or in sub-standard conditions.

No matter which type of job you want, be sure to look at every aspect of the job and life you are being offered, rather than being wooed solely by a high salary. If it sounds too good to be true, it probably is. Look out for suspicious language, lack of information, any agent or employer that is bullying you or pushing you to do something that seems wrong, or refusals to provide the correct paperwork for a Z working visa. Additionally, never trust a recruiter, whether Chinese or an agent in your home country, that wants to charge you for their services. Job placement in Chinese schools should always be free. [1]

Job hunting

There are two basic ways to find a teaching gig in China. The first is to set out onto the internet on your own and weed through hundreds of job ads, school websites and Chinese recruiters. The other way is to go through a placement agency in your home country or a recruiter in China. Either way, you'll be asked to provide a list of documents, which you should prepare beforehand. This will probably involve some scanning. As well, it is always helpful if your resume lists some teaching experience, as many provincial governments will refuse working permits to job applicants without such experience (though the schools themselves do not usually require experienced teachers). Before starting your job hunt, it would be wise to prepare the following documents:

---

[1] May not apply if you are participating in a volunteer short-term program.

- **Resume** – should list your date of birth, nationality, birthplace and highlight the fact that you are a native English speaker, as well as display your teaching experience.
- **Color photo** – a recent color photo to process your work permit.
- **Degree** – a scan/image of your highest-level degree.
- **TEFL certificate** – a scan/image of your TEFL or teaching cert

A couple of optional but potentially useful documents to have on hand are:
- **Letter of reference** from your most recent employer or student
- **Health certificate** – a basic travel medical certificate is useful and sometimes required by the local embassy to issue your visa. A full physical exam, including blood work and X-rays, will be done at your school's expense after you arrive, so don't pay lots of money for a big exam. Just a quick doctor's note will suffice.

On your own

If you're job hunting on your own, first set some serious time aside with Google. There are many websites that offer posting boards and listings, such as Dave's ESL Café (www.eslcafe.com). Other sites like ChinaJob (www.chinajob.com) and TeachCN (www.teachcn.com) offer China-specific job listings and a chance to upload your resume to be found by employers. Be careful, because Chinese recruiters often advertize these jobs in lieu of the schools themselves, and Chinese recruiters are not the most trustworthy sources.

It is all-too-easy to be duped by a scammer-recruiter or fake school that will string you along with excellent promises for several weeks and then drop a bomb like, "We can't get your Z visa in time. Come on a tourist visa". Generally these schools rely on making money by employing foreign teachers illegally for a few months, by-passing their legal (and expensive) obligation to become licensed to hire foreigners. This particular scenario has happened to me personally, so be aware that it can happen to almost anyone, and never fully trust an offer until you have the visa documents in your hands.

A few rules of thumb:

- Never trust a recruiter or employer that doesn't give you all of the information up front, including the contract, working hours, accommodation and visa information.
- Never, EVER agree to enter China to teach on an L tourist visa.
- Look out for recruiters/employers that use vague language, don't respond to you right away or use very poor, broken English.
- Do not let a recruiter or school try to convince you that an activity you believe to be illegal is "OK in this situation" or "legal in this case".
- Never give money to a recruiter to find you a job or sign a contract that stipulates part of your salary go to recruitment fees.
- Do not trust a recruiter or school that asks you to come to China personally for an interview. Do not spend money making long distance calls – they should call you.

Home-country placement agencies

A good few agencies now exist in Western countries to help place ESL teachers into jobs in Asia. These can be decent options if you are a beginner ESL teacher with no idea about finding a job in China. Many times, these agencies have stiffer requirements and more stringent interview processes than the schools themselves would conduct. As well, you may not get as much say in where you are placed geographically as you would by job hunting on your own. However, your odds of being taken advantage of or falling prey to a scam are less than if you were finding a job on your own via the internet.

Keep in mind that you should never pay for the services of a home country placement agency. Look for one that offers you a range of options in terms of possible placements and be sure to ask about things like working hours, public vs. private schools, salary, holidays, accommodation and benefits. A good placement agency will keep you in the loop the entire time and give you access to all information about your future employer. They should also help with the signing of the contract, which they should grant you access to before you arrive in China. Some placement agencies help handle flights and other travel arrangements (though you'll be responsible for those costs).

One final reminder – religious proselytizing is illegal and punishable in China. While it is a noble idea to reach out to others in need around the world, it is generally a very *bad* idea to engage in illegal activity that could result in fines or imprisonment. When choosing a placement agency, recruiter or school, be careful to ensure that they have no ulterior motives or subversive agenda, religious or otherwise.

Getting Out

The following information is provided in the context of United States visa processing. If you are not a U.S. citizen, check with the Chinese embassy in your home country for the correct process to obtaining a Chinese visa. Generally speaking, a Chinese visa must be obtained at the Chinese embassy or consulate in your home country before you depart. If you are a U.S. citizen living abroad, depending on your situation, you can either apply at the local Chinese embassy or utilize a visa agency to process your paperwork in the United States via overnight shipping (contact your local Chinese embassy to find out which option you should take).

Passport – 护照 hùzhào

To travel to China, you'll need two things. The first is a passport from your home country, valid for *at least* as long as you'll be staying abroad. If you've never traveled abroad before and don't currently have a passport, you'll need to apply for one through your country's appropriate government agency. United States citizens can apply for a passport at authorized post offices throughout the U.S. You'll have to fill out an application form, show proof of citizenship (a birth certificate, social security card, etc), and bring two passport photos. Passport photos can be taken at Walgreen's (or other pharmacies), AAA, and most travel agencies. You can get more info about obtaining a U.S. passport on the web at: travel.state.gov.

Visa – 签证 qiānzhèng

You also need a visa to visit China. This is an official permit, attached to your passport, allowing entry into and travel within a particular country or region. Visas are issued by the embassy or consulate of the country to which you'll be traveling (in this case, China). If you don't get the proper visa before arriving, you may be turned away at immigration (迁居移民 qiānjū yímín). Needless to say, visas are incredibly important. There are many types of visas for foreigners coming to China.

Chinese Visas by Type

- **L Visa**: A 30-day visa for tourism, family visits or personal matters.
- **F Visa**: These are business visas issued to people invited for business, research, lecture, short-term studies or internships for *no more than six months*. Some provinces let foreign teachers work on F visas under contracts shorter than six months.
- **X Visa**: A student visa issued for the purpose of study or intern practice for a period of *more than six months*.
- **Z Visa**: A work visa issued to those hired by Chinese companies to work or teach in China, including accompanying family members. Foreign teachers heading to China for a year must obtain a Z Visa.
- **G Visa**: Issued for transit through China. American passport holders must obtain a transit visa to fly through all Chinese airports except Pudong International Airport in Shanghai.
- **D Visa**: Issued to applicant who is to reside permanently in China.

If you are a…

…backpacker visiting China on holidays, you need an L visa.
…student doing a semester abroad in China, you need an F visa.
…student doing a year abroad in China, you need an X visa.
…individual invited to teach or work in China, you need a Z visa.
…traveler getting a connecting flight, you need a G visa.
…hoping to stay in China permanently, you need a D visa.

There has been a lot of hubbub about 'multiple entry' visas, or visas that allow you to leave and enter China more than once. If you're just going to China on holiday, the odds of getting a multi-entry visa are very slim. It might be possible to obtain them through travel agencies in Hong Kong, but don't rely solely on that. It is also possible to be granted a visa extension once you are on the ground in China. You must turn up at a local Public Security Bureau (PSB) - aka the police station - and explain your situation. It might be helpful to bring along a Chinese speaker for this.

The Elusive Z Visa

The Z visa is granted to all foreigners coming to China for work, including long-term foreign teachers. To get a Z visa, you first need a letter of invitation from the school or company where you'll be working, along with a foreign expert certificate and work permit from the provincial and local governments where you'll be living. Your school or recruitment agency will take care of this for you and should express mail these necessary documents to you from China after you've been offered a job. You will need these documents, as well as your passport and several small photos, when you apply for the Z visa at the Chinese embassy in your home country.

After you've arrived in China, you'll get a passport stamp at passport control in the airport. Within a week or two, your school will help you register with the local police station, the Public Security Bureau (PSB). They will give you white slip of paper that serves as temporary registration of your presence in town. A week or two later, your passport will be turned in to the local PSB headquarters in application for your Foreign Residence Permit. As things go in China, your passport could be 'held hostage' there for god knows how long. If it's gone for more than a week, bug your school officials to hurry it up. The PSB will void your Z visa (which was only useful to get you *in to* the country), and attach a new document – your Foreign Residence Permit (居留证 jūliú zhèng). This permit, which looks very similar to a visa, is what will allow you to legally stay within China for a period of up to 12 months. Incidentally, the permit allows you to enter and exit China as many times as you wish. So, fear not! You can return home or travel abroad during holidays with no trouble!

Applying for a visa in the U.S. is not difficult. The Chinese embassy is located in Washington D.C. and there are five additional consulates in Chicago, Houston, Los Angeles, New York and San Francisco. If you happen to live in or near any of those cities, you can take the necessary documents and apply in-person. In that case, it will take between 3 to 5 days to process your visa. Rush services are available for an extra fee, allowing your visa to be processed within one or two days.

If you do not live in one of those cities, you'll need to submit your documentation to a paid visa service. This service will charge an additional fee (on top of the actual visa fee paid to the Chinese consulate) to run your stuff over to the consulate, obtain the visa, and mail it all back to you. The process takes a little longer, but can usually be rushed at an extra cost - should be about a week altogether. Scour the internet for a reputable paid visa service that offers a decent price (around $200 with shipping).

It is important to note once more that entering China on an L tourist visa and expecting to work is both illegal and potentially dangerous. Any school or recruitment agency that asks you to enter China on such conditions is probably not licensed to hire foreigners by the State Administration for Foreign Expert Affairs (SAFEA). A reputable, licensed school will always provide you with the necessary documentation to obtain a Z visa before arriving in China.

Packing

No matter which way you look at it, packing is a nightmare. Whether you are backpacking through China, doing a short-term program, or moving for a year-long contract, packing will no doubt be at the top of your list of overwhelming pre-trip activities. Fear not! I've compiled a list of packing must-haves and things you'll definitely want to consider taking along. Bear in mind, *many* basic daily necessities can be purchased easily (and cheaply!) in China. Consider leaving behind smaller, throw-away items such as toiletries and DVDs, which can easily be purchased after your arrival.

STUFF TO BRING

- **Clothes that fit!** Unless you're petite, it'll be difficult to buy clothes in China. Take loose fitting clothes that you don't mind wearing out.
- **Comfy shoes!** Bring two pairs: everyday and dressy. Flip-flops or sandals are also handy. You *can* buy shoes in China, unless you have massive feet, though tall women might be forced into buying men's shoes and should be prepared for strange looks from shopkeepers!
- **First-aid Kit!** Include cold remedies you prefer, rubbing alcohol or hydrogen peroxide, band-aids, some over-the-counter pain pills, allergy remedies, anti-diarrheal and a thermometer.
- **Re-freezable ice pack**! These aren't available in China and you never know when something strange is going to happen. One time I woke up with a bizarre fat lip and had to ice it with a pack of dumplings...
- **Tampons**! Ladies, bring *enough* and I do mean enough. Tampons are hard to find and the ones that are on hand don't have applicators. Yuck.
- **Deodorant!** Some supermarkets have small, semi-useless sticks of deodorant, but bring several of your favorite brand to be safe.
- **Sunscreen**! It's hard to find, expensive, contains bleaching agent and usually only comes in tiny bottles. Stock up on the Banana Boat, people!
- **Coats! Jackets! Raincoats!** These types of things *are* available but *probably won't* fit you. Bring your own and something warm for winter.
- **Undergarments**! Once again, come armed with your own! As a U.S. size 12, I once had to buy an XXXL maternity bra in China.
- **English materials!** Novels, books, texts, maps, etc for class materials.
- **China Travel Guide!** The Rough Guide and Lonely Planet are staples.
- **Can opener!** I was once reduced to opening an aluminum can using a wine corkscrew, a butter knife, and a chopstick. It wasn't pretty.
- **Ice trays**! You'll have a freezer, so bring trays or those magic baggies.
- **Cooking spices**! Dried herbs and spices like garlic salt, basil, oregano, cinnamon and black pepper come in very handy!
- **Photos! Reminders of home**! You'll be glad for a few tokens when you are far away, and they can also make for fun class material.

What to Wear

For teaching, casual but modest dress is fine. The key is to be comfortable, especially for those traveling to hotter southern areas with less air conditioning. Shorts are fine for men and women (though don't blame me if you get stared at more than usual for showing off your white legs), but women should take care to have a modest length. Breathable fabrics that dry quickly, like cotton and linen, are sensible. Also, bring *at least* one dressy outfit for banquet dinners, ceremonies, and evenings out and at least one pair of comfortable shoes for walking and standing.

Rain gear is essential, especially in coastal areas, though umbrellas and ponchos are cheap and everywhere. You could bring a swimsuit, although swimming is not popular in China. There are very few beaches and Chinese people fear the sun and avoid tanning. The few beaches that do exist in China are overrun with confused tourists wearing leisure suits and high heels, staring at the water with befuddled amusement, or hiding from the sun under newspapers and plastic bags. Places like Hainan Island and other coastal areas might provide some swimming time. Be wary though – the waters in China's seas are unusually polluted and perhaps not safe.

My luggage is too heavy!

For me, packing is a total and utter nightmare. Trying to cram my entire life into 20 kilos makes me want to curl up on the kitchen floor and drink merlot from the bottle. Thankfully, I've learned a few things over the years, mostly from awful experiences (like that time I had to abandon an *entire suitcase* in the Shanghai airport...).

Firstly, your entire life just isn't going to fit into 20 kilos, so don't even think about it. If you don't have a friendly attic or local storage locker, you're going to have to part with some stuff. Start by dividing your going-to-China stuff into things that you absolutely need when you first hit the ground (like clothes) and things that aren't so urgent (like that decorative carpet or your ultra-hip cowboy boots). Go out and get a decently sized shipping box and cram as much as you can into it. You'll need a luggage scale (check Walmart) to try the weight, and that will come in handy later when you're packing up the ole suitcase. You also need to get on the horn (or the 'net) to find out your future mailing address. It will probably be sent to you in Chinese characters, which you'll print and paste onto the box. Pack it up a few days before your departure and check the weight. It shouldn't be more than about a hundred bucks. To save some cash, don't express mail it - you've got time.

Non-urgent stuff dealt with, now you've got to attend to the luggage. Doing this has honestly sent me spiraling into bouts of insomnia before. *Will it be too heavy? What if I have to throw out my grandma's scarves?* (Hint: you might want to consider stuffing granny's scarves into that friendly attic).

You need to come to terms with the fact that you'll probably have to part with some stuff. Thus prepared, make the most out of your space by bringing garments that you can combine into several outfits, rather than *all your jeans*. Give some stuff to charity or let your niece make cutoffs. Whatever, just PARE DOWN. Here are a few tips and tricks that have helped me kill the packing blues and ditch the airport hassles in the past.

- Stick spices into labeled baggies and toss the bottles. Glass is heavy!
- Wear heavy stuff on the plane, & carry your coat & laptop.
- Pack the heaviest stuff (like books) into your carry-on luggage. Carry-ons are vastly under-used, so cram, cram cram, people!
- While we're at it, don't bring too many books. They are *so* heavy.
- Don't bring liquid toiletries. You can get shampoo in China.
- Use shrink-wrap bags to allow for more space in your luggage.
- Give away your hair dryer. You can get one when you arrive.
- Line your guitar case with socks and underwear. (I actually did this!)
- Your printer, ceiling fan and DVD collection are non-essential items.
- So are your ski boots.
- Pack and repack several times until you get it right!

Chapter 3
Arrival & Daily life

Culture Shock

Arriving to a new country is never easy – it can run the traveler through an emotional ringer. One may experience ups, downs, highs and lows and many emotions are heightened to their extremes. You should not overlook culture shock and the adaptation stages, especially when first arriving in a foreign country to live for a long duration.

Sociologists and cultural specialists agree that culture shock and adaptation take on several stages, which were first outlined by the anthropologist Kalvero Oberg in the early 1900s. It is important to recognize these stages for what they are and to maintain a healthy level of self-awareness as you begin to learn about life in China. Particularly during the stages where negative emotions are intensified, it is important to keep culture shock in mind as a contributing factor. Also bear in mind that everyone reacts differently to the changes and experiences of living in a different cultural environment. No two experiences are exactly the same, but the following stages will give you a framework for gauging your feelings.

Stage 1: *Elated Phase* – First 1-3 months. Everything in the new culture seems amazing, positive emotions are heightened and every new experience is interesting and pleasing. At times, you may even feel euphoric as you explore the contrasts and idiosyncrasies of the new culture. At this point, you will find the Chinese propensity for staring and honking rather cute and endearing.

Stage 2: *Irritation Phase* – 2-6 months. Problems suddenly begin to occur. Small details seem more consequential and difficulties feel concentrated. You may perceive the locals as unfriendly, or feel that the most menial tasks, such as shopping or eating, represent a crisis. You may experience feelings of loneliness, isolation, unhappiness, depression, or anger during this stage, and the language barrier represents a serious problem. At this point, you will find the Chinese propensity for staring and honking so maddening that you want to poke someone's eye out.

Stage 3: *Adjustment Phase* – After 3-6 months. During this phase, you will feel a renewed interest in the host culture. You begin to understand small things about the new culture and feel more confident maneuvering in daily life. You feel a fresh fondness toward the culture and a second happiness with your life. The language barrier lessens as you understand more of the local speech. At this point, you will find the Chinese propensity for staring and honking annoying, but not life ending.

Stage 4: *Integration Phase* – Usually after 6 months or more. In this phase you finally feel at home in the new culture. You can maneuver through daily activities without problems and never feel a sense of dread or unease about small tasks. You make friends and have confidence with basic activities, and you're able to use local speech for all necessary activities. You understand that both your home and host cultures have good and bad things to offer and you are confident in your new life. At this point, you will still find the Chinese propensity for staring and honking annoying because it NEVER STOPS BEING ANNOYING! But other things, like eating and shopping, are easy as pie.

Stage 5: *Re-entry Phase* – This phase only occurs after the traveler has spent a significant amount of time away from home. Upon return, you feel a sense of change within yourself as you look at your home culture through a new set of international glasses. The most difficult part of the Re-entry Phase is that the change within yourself is not reflected in your home culture. Your friends and family may not 'get it', while life has simply gone on in your absence. Additionally, things about your culture or home may have changed. The customs you've adopted in the new country no longer apply back home, and you may experience feelings of confusion and isolation as you are suddenly expected to return to old cultural habits.

One key to overcoming culture shock is to recognize it as it happens. By knowing yourself and understanding the root of your emotions, you will be able to battle unnecessary feelings of depression and frustration. It's also a good idea to take time for yourself, especially during Stage 2, when you may be feeling particularly frustrated or irritated by the new culture.

Alone time is especially important for Westerners and it is one of the biggest difficulties faced by laowai. With Chinese cultural norms relying heavily on group time, we Westerners initially feel exhausted and emotionally spent from the amount of time in the company of others. Spend evenings reading a book or enjoying a movie at home. Go out for walks alone, try cooking or take a short weekend trip.

Equally important is to make friends in the new culture, which will allow you to get out, have dinner and try some local customs. Also, it will benefit you to seek refuge with other foreigners, if possible. You will do yourself an incredible service by sharing the difficulties and pleasantries of life in China with other laowai. The quicker you adapt to new cultural norms, the better off you will be!

Logistics

Banks - 银行 yínháng

Your school should help you secure a bank account (银行帐户 yínháng zhànghù). If you are arrived several weeks and still have no account, talk to your Foreign Expert Officer (FEO - your assigned school representative) or an

English speaker to help you with the necessary paperwork. You will be required to show your passport and some proof of employment, which should be taken care of by your school or employer. Banks in China operate very similarly to foreign banks, but be aware that they will likely issue you a 'passbook' (存簿 cúnbù) to your account, which you should carry if you plan to make withdrawals (提款 tíkuǎn) or deposits (存钱 cúnqián).

It's easier to do most of your banking via ATM (提款机 tíkuǎn jī), especially if your Chinese is limited. Some schools offer a direct deposit salary system, while others pay each month in cash. It will depend on your school as to how and when you are paid, but monthly is the most common system. Most of the major Chinese banks are recommendable; Bank of China, China Construction Bank, Bank of Agriculture, or The Industrial and Commercial Bank of China all have branches nationwide with plenty of ATMs available.

China is mostly a cash economy. You will be issued an ATM card with your bank account, but credit/debit card (信用卡 xìnyòngkǎ) use is only starting to become common, so don't count on one for daily shopping. Your ATM card will work as a debit card at department stores or supermarkets through a localized system called Union Pay. If you see the Union Pay symbol you can use your ATM to debit in that store. You *can't* use it to shop online or anywhere outside Mainland China, nor can you withdraw from an ATM outside of Mainland China.

If you have a credit/debit card from home that you wish to access, you can do so through ATMs at many major banks. But beware, banking is still developing in China and many kinks have yet to be worked out. You might find your card inexplicably rejected from five machines and suddenly work in the 6th for no apparent reason. TIC!

Cell Phones (手机 shǒujī)

Having a mobile phone is pertinent in China. Even some of the poorest people still spring for phones and Chinese people value phone contact. There are two major mobile providers in China: China Mobile and China Unicom. China Mobile is the larger of the two and tends to be more reliable, although service ranges with both providers are very good. It's rare to experience connectivity problems throughout eastern China.

There are hundreds of different service plans to choose from and specials change by the month. The only recommendable way to choose a cell phone plan is to bring along a Chinese friend, coworker, or school representative to explain everything. Generally, mobile accounts operate on a pay-as-you-go basis rather than contractually. Under this system, you purchase the phone and SIM card (which includes your phone number) and simply add money to the account as you need it.

International Dialing

Making international calls via mobile phone can be extremely difficult. I've had mixed success with calling home, even on plans that were promised to have IDD (international dialing). Additionally, there is often difficulty with international text messaging (SMS). Sometimes you can't communicate internationally by text, sometimes only receive texts, and sometimes only send them! TIC!

If you sign up for a pay-as-you-go plan, you will need to drop in to the local office or branch of your cell provider to 'add money' (jiā fèi 加费) to your phone. The major providers offer information numbers to check the amount left and often SMS messages will arrive when your account is low on money. Once inside the office, you will need to ask where to add money and provide your phone number and name. If you aren't good at speaking yet, write your number down for the sales person. They will ask how much you wish to pay (nǐ fù/jiā dōu shǎo? 你 付/ 加都 少?) and you can hand over the cash.
Chinese cell service is also riddled with spam text messages. Several times a day, you may receive random texts in Chinese that can be ignored. You might also receive welcome/farewell messages when leaving or entering your local service area.

Finally, it's worth mentioning that Chinese phone culture differs greatly from that of most Western cultures. In China, it's considered very rude not to answer a phone call at any time. It's perfectly acceptable to interrupt a meeting, class or dinner with phone calls, and your Chinese friends may feel very offended if they are unable to reach you by phone. Occasionally, you may have a persistent acquaintance or student that calls you dozens of times in a row. This can be extremely difficult to handle at first, but you will learn to adjust to Chinese phone culture. I work to train my friends about my personal phone habits, in that I value not answering calls during dinners or important meetings. Don't feel slighted if they do, but explain that this is why they may not be able to reach you at certain times. It is also recommendable to keep your mobile phone numbers fairly private, otherwise you will probably receive handfuls of vague text messages from unnamed students: "hi teacher. what u doing? i am your student." and so on. While this may be cute once or twice, it can wears down your phone money (and your patience) quickly.

Internet & Computers – 网 *wǎng* & 电脑 *diànnǎo*

Your school should provide an internet connection in your apartment, which might be paid either by the school or individually by you. If you don't have a laptop, your school should also provide a desktop. Though, be forewarned: Chinese computers are often old, pieced together, and slow! If you have the means, bring along your own laptop (this will also be useful for photo storage).

Even though DSL and Broadband are normal, their connections aren't necessarily fast or reliable. Unfortunately, you'll simply have to adjust to slow, fluctuating connections, unloadable pages and other problems. Additionally, there is the issue of the 'Great Firewall', the Chinese government's attempt to censor the internet using filters that block certain websites. At various times in the past, Wikipedia, BBC, Flickr, YouTube, Twitter and others have been unreachable, as well as many .co.uk and .gov extensions, several major blogging sites (like Blogger and WordPress). It will depend on when you're there. You can use a proxy (use Google to find one) to access blocked sites.

Using the internet to stay in touch with family and friends back home is still reliable, nonetheless. It is worthwhile to download the latest versions of programs like Skype, AIM, Yahoo, or others that will allow you to use free voice chat. You can purchase cheap headsets to converse with people anywhere via your computer for free. The connections are good enough to support this kind of chat, and you can also buy a webcam for video chat. This is the most reliable, accessible way to keep in touch internationally, so get your family and friends back home on the voice chat bandwagon!

In larger cities, free wireless hotspots are becoming more and more common. Small coffee shops and Westerner cafés often boast wifi hotspots or internet connections for your laptop. Likewise, internet cafés (网吧 wǎngbā) abound, even in smaller towns, so you will never be without connection of some kind. If you are backpacking, you might bring along or buy a portable headset, as many hostels and internet cafes offer Skype.

If you are teaching, your students may try to entice you to use a program called QQ. Beware! QQ is a chat program used mostly in China and some other areas of Asia. Like MSN or AIM, QQ requires you to download software from the internet onto your machine. Unfortunately, QQ is riddled with adware, spyware, and lots of viruses. If you decide to try it (first of all, GOOD LUCK navigating the website to even figure out how to download it in the first place), use it at your own risk. **I do not recommend putting QQ onto your personal computer.** Additionally, there have been several reports of QQ identities being stolen or hacked. The general recommendation is to stay away!

A final note about using Chinese computers for those unfamiliar with the language: The computers provided by your school or those found in internet bars will probably have their languages set to Chinese. Oftentimes, it's difficult or impossible to change the language settings, so you'll have to get used to using the computer as it is. Look at the dropdown menus: you can see a letter next to the Chinese characters. Often, that letter represents the command as it would be in English. For instance, 'D' on the menu means 'delete'. These letters can help you find your way.

Chinese computers also have a setting that allows you to switch the typing text between Chinese and English, or using Roman letters to type Chinese characters by first searching the pinyin. Usually, to switch back and forth on the Windows Language Bar, you press Shift + Alt. At the bottom right of your screen, near or in the task tray, you'll see a small icon with EN or CH, or a tiny keyboard icon. If you find yourself inexplicably unable to type in English, or a strange menu bar pops up offering Chinese characters, you have probably been switched to the Chinese type function. Use the Shift + Alt command or click on that icon in the task bar to revert to English.

Daily Living

Your Apartment - 公寓 gōngyù

Most teachers' living quarters are on-campus apartments, or occasionally off-campus housing near the school. You can expect basic accommodation with 3-4 rooms, a hard bed, a TV and DVD player, desk, small table and chairs, and a cramped kitchen. In most cases, the bathroom will have a Western-style seater potty with an open shower that empties into a small floor drain in the middle of the room (instead of a shower stall), and sometimes the laundry machine will also be located in the bathroom or kitchen.

Many times, foreign teacher housing is a block of apartments designated for foreign teachers each year, or grouped with other Chinese teachers' housing. Therefore, your flat will be pretty well used and definitely not new, and maybe not that clean when you move in. Furthermore, it can be really difficult to keep clean, as you track in loads of grime on your person, especially your feet, which makes the Chinese habit of removing shoes in the house very useful.

Laundry (衣物 yīwù)

Some type of laundry facility or service will be available. Though a washing machine (洗衣机 xǐyī jī) may be present, a tumble dryer usually isn't, so clothes will be hung to dry. It could be useful to bring along clothespins and a line if you are backpacking. Otherwise, laundry services are available in most hostels and hotels. If you are moving to China for a longer stint, you'll likely have a washing machine and drying pole in your apartment, though you'd be well advised to get an English-speaking local to explain the washing machine functions! It's not necessary to bring an iron, as hanging clothes to dry means not dealing with wrinkles (if you're desperate for an iron, you can buy them in supermarkets)! Washing detergent and fabric softener can be procured easily in markets and small shops.

Don't come expecting your clothes to be soft and dry like they would at home. The general humidity levels make drying difficult and often clothes are still semi-damp, even after hours in direct sunlight. It can also be arduous to get things smelling clean, but one trick is to use more detergent than you would normally at home. Also, splash out for Tide or another name brand. The extra two or three yuan every few months isn't going to break your bank, but it might just make the difference in how clean your clothing smells!

Shopping - 买东西 mǎi dōngxī

Shopping in China can be a bit of an adventure! Very often, prices are negotiable, so never accept a tag amount. Bargaining can be done with the help of a translator or student, and many merchants use a calculator to exchange price offers with foreigners. Bargaining is particularly common in commodities markets or small shops, while prices in supermarkets and up market stores are fixed. When shopping in tourist or sightseeing areas, never accept a tag amount.

You may also notice that merchants or workers are keen to help you, give you advice or offer you items you really don't want. In another aspect of the collective Chinese mindset, average people rely on this kind of advice during shopping or ordering. If you don't like or want the item, simply shake your head or say "No, thanks." [不要. 谢谢 bú yào, xìe xie.]. You may also very directly say that you don't like it or you prefer another color. It's best to be assertive and direct. Take a nod from the Chinese shoppers – they will always speak their minds openly and usually take charge!

TIC Bargaining Rules of Thumb

- Decide on the highest amount you'll pay *before* you begin shopping.
- Lowball your first offer. Cut the merchant's first price in half.
- Let the merchant retort with a lower price each time you raise yours.
- Bargain upwards in small increments, depending on the item.
- Never look too interested in the item. If she thinks you want it, she'll hardball the price.
- Walk away, even if you think you'll buy it. Lead the merchant to believe the item isn't special and she'll come down. She might even chase you!
- Upon purchase, be friendly. Even after all that bargaining, she'll probably happily give you change and send you on your way with a 'thank you.' Probably not before trying to sell you some other crap you don't need, though! This is China, after all.

Business Cards – 名片 míngpiàn

Business cards (or 'name cards') are all the rage in China. It is customary to exchange cards during formal introductions, so if you have a card, be sure to carry several with you. If you don't already have one, you can easily have one made after you arrive. Chinese card and banner shops will usually do a bilingual card with English on one side and Chinese on the other. These types of cards are extremely common among laowai and Chinese alike.

Card exchanging culture is precise, but fear not – it's difficult to offend someone too severely with a card. When exchanging cards, offer yours with both hands and face the writing toward the recipient (Chinese-side up!). Also, receive cards with both hands and do not put the card directly in your pocket or purse - that's rude. It is more polite to leave the card out on the table or in hand for a few minutes. Having a card can also facilitate exchanging contact information with your students, who will inevitably wish to keep in touch!

A word of caution to teachers – be careful about exchanging information with your students. It may sound cynical to you now, but you will understand later when 400 eager students have your mobile phone number and while the night away sending text messages. It's especially important for those going to small towns (i.e. any town that isn't a provincial capital), to keep their personal contact information somewhat private. Believe me, word will spread about your existence and you'll probably be the local celebrity before long. So, unless you yearn for awkward phone conversations with students whose names you can't remember or unannounced home visits on your Sunday morning off, it's really better to keep your contact info on the DL.

Massage Parlor - 按摩院 *ànmó yuàn*

There are two kinds of massage parlors in China, one offering straightforward massage, and the other offering *more* to the discerning patron. This second type is referred to as a 'red lantern' and often comes disguised as a small, shoddy hair salon. In the evenings, these salons glow a dim red or blue light from within, and you can usually spot bored-looking girls sitting around or calling to potential patrons from the front stoop.

Normal massage parlors look much more legitimate and usually have a fairly ornate lobby area with a reception desk and uniformed staff. You can specify which type of massage you want - foot, back, shoulder, etc - and pay accordingly. You are then led upstairs to private rooms with one to three large sofa chairs for your comfort. With a foot massage, you'll usually get a hot herbal foot soak while trained masseuses work on your shoulders and back. During and after the massage, you may also be treated to snacks, dumplings or tea. Evenings are a great time to get a massage, and it can be a lovely social activity with one or two friends.

Chinese massage is not for the faint of heart. Traditional Chinese medicine suggests that massage should be rigorous to promote circulation, so, masseuses are trained to poke and prod you with extreme vigor. If it's too intense, ask the masseuse to lighten his or her touch (qīng yī diǎn 轻一点).

Hair Salon 理发店 lǐfà diàn

A trip to the hair salon can be either incredibly pleasant or absolutely horrifying. On the plus side, Chinese hair salons are incredibly cheap and the staff is always friendly and excited to meet a laowai. On the negative side, hair stylists in China are simply not trained nor accustomed to dealing with foreign hair. Especially if you have curly hair, you should be careful until you develop a working relationship with your stylist or else things might end in disaster. One major rule of thumb when getting your haircut: be flexible. Go in expecting the unexpected. It's entirely possible you will find a great stylist who does a magnificent job on your hair. But really, TIC right?

The mechanics of the salon are fairly straightforward and very similar to Western salons. You won't need to schedule an appointment because walk-ins are normal. You can opt for a simple shampoo (洗头发 xǐ tóufa), cut (剪头发 jiǎn tóufa), or a dye job (染色 rǎnsè). Salons are often open very late at night; so many Chinese women make a social outing with friends to have their hair washed. Even if you just go for a shampoo, you'll be treated to a head and neck massage, as well as an ear cleaning and an eyebrow/beard trimming. So, going in for a ¥10 shampoo really is worthwhile.

Interestingly, the shampoo is administered dry. A young stylist will wash your hair as you sit in the chair, using shampoo and a small water squirt bottle. After a vigorous head massage, she will rinse your hair in a sink chair and return you to the regular chair for your neck and arm massage. After you are duly relaxed (or in pain), the cut will commence. Most salons are equipped with plenty of magazines to choose a cut, but if you have a particular style in mind, take a photo with you.

If you want to get your hair colored, you'll be presented with a tablet full of color samples to choose from. Keep in mind, the colors are usually bright and meant for Chinese hair, so the results on a laowai head can sometimes be amusing, strange, or aggravating. Furthermore, the colors on the tablets almost never really match the colors that come out on your hair. Rule of thumb: choose a discreet, simple color. The language barrier is difficult and, often, ideas about hair styling are lost in translation, especially since the stylists are usually trained in a few specific cuts at a vocational or training school. The way to survive is to simply be flexible. Whatever happens, it will eventually grow out! TIC!

Post Office – 邮电局 yóudiàn jú

Chinese post is a lot like other Chinese bureaucracies – slow and unreliable. Domestic mail is fairly cheap, while international mail varies depending on the service you choose. China Post utilizes EMS Courier Service, which provides a tracking number and is quite reliable for international express delivery; but it isn't cheap. Sending (寄 jì) via normal post is anything *but* express. Packages will arrive anywhere from two weeks to more than a month later, possibly having been delivered by donkey. Likewise, packages arriving from abroad via normal post could take up to two months, despite what post offices may guarantee back home. Once on Chinese soil, all bets are off! Packages may be opened, inspected, quarantined, damaged, or simply lost.

Mail boxes (邮筒 yóutǒng) are green and usually located in conspicuous spots, like the fronts of post offices. Inside the post office, you are at the mercy of individual postal workers who, really, have way too much power. You aren't likely to run into too many problems, but go in expecting just about anything. If you are turned away or told "no," don't take it as a final answer. Bring a friend to help bargain/translate, ask again several times, return on another day, or try a different post office until you succeed!

Teachers are generally provided a mailing address (地质 dìzhǐ) at their schools where packages (包裹 bāoguǒ) and letters (信 xìn) can be sent. In larger cities, the postal service *should* be able to handle mail addressed in pinyin (Chinese written in Roman letters). Once again, though, TIC. If you want to play it safe, have a Chinese colleague email you the address written in Chinese characters and convert it to an image or PDF. Then, have your friends/family at home print the image and paste it to the front of the package or letter. Also, be sure to also provide them your address written out in pinyin lettering for the customs form (my mother was once forced to try writing Chinese characters on a custom form - not pretty!) Doing all this, you up the chances of receiving your mail accurately.

Chapter 4
On Being an FT...
"So, you're a teacher?'
"Apparently, I am now!'

Foreigners come to teach English (教英语 jiāo yīngyǔ) in China for many reasons and most of them have little to do with an actual interest in being a teacher (老师 lǎoshī). A good portion of foreign teachers (FTs) (外教 wàijiào) have little-to-no experience in the classroom, which really ends up fine because the vast majority of teachers are hired to present oral English classes. If you have been hired to teach reading and writing, the odds are that you have *some* prior experience teaching English, so the classroom should be no stranger to you.

This information was gleaned from dozens of teachers' experiences, varying from public to private schools, university to elementary ages, in several different provinces across China. The idea here is to offer you an idea of **what to expect** when you first arrive in the classroom and a **teaching game plan** so you can hit the ground running. From there, you can find your way. And if you happen to wake up one morning, groggy and hungover with no plan for the next three hours of classes, there are some helpful suggestions and useful games that will hopefully make your life a little easier.

What to Expect

Chinese classrooms (教室 jiàoshì) can be a bit of a shock to any system, even veteran teachers. Although, in some ways, students are students (学生 xuésheng) and many of the problems you encounter are not unlike those you would deal with in any classroom across the world, working with Chinese students presents unique challenges.

A good rule of thumb is to think of yourself less as an English teacher and more as a cultural liaison. Meaning, if you think of your job as to cross cultural boundaries and foster an interest in English among your students, you will be better off than if you try to shove spelling and grammar down their throats. Incidentally, depending on their ages and grade levels, their written English grammar may nearly be as good as yours. Plus, your students will probably have 2-5 English classes in addition to their weekly oral classes with you, which absolves you from shouldering the entire burden of English instruction. Good news for those of us who have trouble remembering back to elementary grammar class! This book sets out to give you a few ways to make your job as a teacher easier, make your workload smaller, and make your classes more fun and interesting. You'll find tips and tricks, classroom games and ways to create lessons (课 kè) without spending hours planning.

Initially, your students will probably be shy and reserved. The education system in China relies on rote memorization and strict classroom protocol, so don't be surprised if they are unwilling to speak up or volunteer at first. It is your job to gain their trust and encourage them to open up. Be assured that they will; it just takes time and effort on your part. It is important to invest in your students, both emotionally and academically, to ensure that they and you enjoy the lessons you teach.

On your first day, you should be provided with a student name list for each class that you are teaching (if not, ask the head teacher or school for it). Generally, these name lists are in Chinese, but you can have the students fill in their English names next to the Chinese names for your benefit.

Additionally, each class might have one student appointed as the 'class monitor'. Class monitors are chosen once a year based on the student's level of maturity and responsibility and their academic achievement. You can use the class monitors to find out information, get supplies and help you keep order in the class. Be sure to ask each class who their monitor is at the outset of the semester.

Teaching Game Plan[1]

Your goal is to get each student to use their English, and ideally, in an oral class setting, to get them to speak out. All kids being equal, some students will be more outgoing and willing to try, while others will remain introverted and shy. Do not expect every student to respond the same way – for one it may be enough to say three words, for others an entire discourse might be reasonable. Use your discretion to cater to each student.

Any sensible means to induce them to use English is fine, as long as you engage them in the language. Utilize your own personal assets and knowledge of the world as a vehicle for their language learning. If you are personally good at science, you could, for example, conduct some easy experiments with them, taking care to incorporate speaking (说 shuō) English into the activity. Likewise, if you are a singer, music may be your vehicle to connect with your students. The possibilities are endless – just go with your strengths and you will be fine. Also, don't be afraid to goof around and have fun with them. Kids are kids and they love to play, so this can be a great way to gain their trust.

Your school (学校 xuéxiào) will probably give you more freedom than most of the Chinese teachers. This means you should be able to come and go from your office (办公室 bàn'gōng shì) or campus at will, rather than being

---

[1] Disclaimer: This book is not a substitute for an accredited, comprehensive course in teaching ESL. To learn an all-purpose approach to EFL instruction, it is best to obtain a professional TEFL/TESL certificate.

chained to your desk all day. With this freedom, however, comes some undue burden. It is not uncommon for schools to simply turn foreign teachers loose on their classes, providing no teaching material whatsoever. If you find yourself faced with a class (班 bān) of students, no book, no lesson, and no material, it is still possible to teach an engaging, interesting lesson on the fly. Perhaps you don't have a textbook (书 shū), but you have all the English in your head and that is enough!

Sample Unit

The following is a sample unit that was used with a Middle School class (ages 12-14). If you have four hours worth of class periods to fill, you could break that time into two units – an hour of listening and an hour of speaking for each. The best way to schedule the units is to use the simple structure of any foreign language course (if you have studied a language, you will know!). Break the units into themes like 'food', 'holidays', 'geography', 'travel', 'My house', etc. Spend the first hour (the listening hour) coming up with vocabulary (have your students help you, they are great with vocabulary words), phrases, and sentences. A few will do, don't take on too many terms. Be sure you write down what you have covered so you can go over it in the next hour and on the exams. Spend some time telling a story or lecture about the theme, using the vocabulary and phrases.

During the second hour (the speaking hour), ask the students questions that utilize the vocabulary and phrases you covered in the previous hour. It is okay to be repetitive and ask each student the same question, as this reinforces what they are learning and allows them to hear and practice on an individual level. It is also a good way to take up time, if you have extra minutes to fill.

The value of a topical approach is that it allows the learner to catalogue new information into mental compartments that are useful later, in context. If your students are more advanced, you can also introduce grammar points into your lessons (one or two per lesson is enough). Centering your lessons topically, rather than basing them on grammar points, gives the learners a context for the language – a kind of situational function for real use.

Unit 5: Travel

Vocabulary
1. Car
2. Plane
3. Train
4. Bus
5. Fly
6. Drive
7. Trip
8. Airport
9. Station
10. Passenger

Phrases
1. Go by car (plane...)
2. Where
3. To go
4. Take a train (bus...)
5. Take off
6. Train/bus station
7. Depart/Arrive
8. Mode of transport

Conversation
1. Where do you want to go?   I want to go to the U.K.
2. How will you get there?   By plane.
3. Where have you been?   I have been to Beijing.
4. How did you get there?   By car.
5. Who goes on a trip?   A passenger.
6. Where do planes take off? At the airport.
7. Where do trains depart?   At the train station.
8. What is your favorite mode of transport?   Train (bus...)

You can become more sophisticated than this, depending on the level of your students. One way to increase the difficulty is to incorporate more/harder vocabulary terms or to have students think of similes for the words (such as boat, ship, etc). Additionally, increasing the length of their response sentences adds complexity. For example:

> *Where do planes take off?*
> Beginner: *Airport*
> Intermediate: *At the airport*
> Advanced: *Planes take off at the airport.*

You could ask more advanced students to write several sentences or paragraphs and recite them for the class, or to discuss the topic in pairs.

You can do this with any number of subjects and it takes very little preparation other than deciding on what theme to cover before each class period. The lessons can be made more interesting by including visual aids for the topics, like photos, maps, books, plants, balloons, etc. Scour the internet for handout material! Local shops carry all kinds of stationary goods, as well as magazines, books, and other supplies.

Choose topics that are interesting to *you*. If you are really into in the subject, you're going to be a much better teacher of it. Think back to your school years – who were the best teachers you had, and why? What made them stand out to you? Your answer will probably have something to do with their enthusiasm and personal investment in the subjects they taught. From the students' point of view, no one wants to listen to and watch a teacher that is bored, unhappy, frowning or blasé. From your point of view, it will be a very long and arduous semester if you can't find a way to engage yourself in the subject matter you're teaching. The topical approach allows you to explore any number of themes that are interesting to you! Speaking from experience, this is incredibly important to having a successful teaching career in China, be it for one month or many years.

Whenever possible, make the students do the work, rather than you. In any given class, there are going to be situations where either a) you can lecture or b) you can let the students self-discover. Believe me, if you talk for 45 (or, god forbid, 90) minutes straight every class period, every week, you will have no voice after two weeks. Let the kids speak up. Reduce the amount of time you spend talking *to* them. Increase the amount of time you *elicit* them to speak to you. Use gestures when possible. Have students write words or phrases on the board, rather than writing everything yourself. Pick out students that are obviously more advanced and use them as interpreters or living dictionaries.

Finally, if you feel like a lesson isn't going well, it probably isn't. If you're bored, the students are definitely bored. So, buck the rules! Don't be afraid to chuck out your lesson plan and create something new on the fly. Throw out the lesson altogether, go outside and play a game of tag!

TIC Teaching Tips

- **Speak slowly** and use **basic vocabulary**. It'll take some practice to condense your thought processes into slower speech, but most students are going to have serious difficulty listening at a native pace.

- Carry a **Chinese/English dictionary** to your classes. You can buy pinyin/English dictionaries in most bookstores in China, or invest in one before you leave. If your students have dictionaries, make them look things up! It creates an air of competition and is good spelling practice.

- Have students do **board work**. Use different colored chalk to represent different things. Category work is very useful for vocabulary terms, such as "Animals with tails," "Animals with four legs," etc. One great game is Pass the Chalk. Choose a student to write one word and give him/her the chalk. Then, let that student pass the chalk to a classmate of choice to write a second word, and that student chooses another, and so on.

- Don't waste time explaining subjects in great detail. The **less wordy**, the better. **Use examples** or **objects** to explain concepts. Repetition with appropriate gesture, example or object should get your point across. Try not to change your wording – that will only add confusion. Stick to one simple grammatical pattern and repeat it.

- ❖ Cater to their level. Figure out what they know initially by asking questions. **Start simple** and move up until they don't understand. Then you'll know their range.

- ❖ **Avoid abstract topics**. Don't try to have discussions about politics, religion, ethics, etc unless your students are very advanced. Abstract topics are difficult to explain and increase the amount of time *you* spend talking *to* them. It's also taboo to discuss religion and politics in school!

- ❖ Use the **chalkboard**! Oftentimes, Chinese students' reading comprehension is far better than their listening comprehension. Just because they don't understand when you *say* the word doesn't mean they don't know the word. If they don't understand, write it on the board!

- ❖ Keep a **list or diary** of all classes and topics covered. With at least five, or sometimes more than ten different class groups to keep track of, you will eventually get confused about what you have covered in a particular class. Keeping a short diary of what you taught each day with each class will help as the semester goes along.

- ❖ **Call roll**. If they don't have English names, assign or let them choose names. This can also be a great icebreaker class on your first day. Make the students write their English names next to their Chinese names on the name list. At the beginning of each class, call roll! The students are terrible at remembering their English names. Calling roll is good practice and also gives a few minutes to ease into English class.

Exams & Grading - 考试 kǎoshì & 考分 kǎofēn

Exams and grading for FT's are kind of a joke. The sad truth is that the school probably doesn't care what grades you give. Your job is mostly to be a figurehead and to give students practice with a native speaker. Even if you *try* to fail a student, the grade will probably be changed after you submit it. To save students' face (and in the larger scheme, the school's reputation), students generally aren't sent home with failing marks from foreign teachers That would reflect badly on everyone, even if the little rugrat deserved to fail!

With that in mind, don't burden yourself with too much grading. Keeping track of dozens of assignments and grades for hundreds of students each semester is going to drive you crazy! My suggestion is to keep track of your best students and learn their names. Give out one or two big assignments (written compositions or in-class speeches are good) and grade them.

In terms of exams, make your life easy. If you've structured your lessons topically (three cheers for the topical approach!), you can simply draw from the topics during an interview-style exam. For instance, if you've covered 'weather', 'travel' and 'music', during your exam, you can ask questions like "Do you like rainy weather? Why/why not?", "Where have you been? Where do you want to go?" and "What is your favorite kind of music? Who is your favorite singer?". The questions and topics will vary depending on your students' levels. However, by doing this, you can simply grade each student on his/her performance during the exam, combined with class participation (do you know their names?), and the one or two big semester assignments to reach a final grade. If you're really good, you can almost keep track in your head. Otherwise, keep a folder with the class name lists, their graded assignments, and the topics you covered in class.

It is frustrating that the grades you give out really aren't worthwhile, but just remember that most of us are in the same boat. Try to look at the bright side: you are free to have fun with your classes in a way that the Chinese teachers are not. You will spend a *lot* less time grading and keeping track of students' marks, which means less work in general. And the real benefit the students have from you is the chance to listen and talk to a native speaker, which will improve their English tenfold. So buck up! You have a rewarding, fun job in a fascinating country! Things could definitely be worse.

Recommendations & Materials

You should prepare some materials in advance to bring with you. Maps, books, art supplies, stickers or other prizes, flashcards and games are all beneficial. Do not go overboard, as your packing space is limited and books are heavy! Art supplies, markers, crayons, colored chalk, construction paper, glue, tape, stickers, ribbons, pins, etc. can all be purchased easily at small shops or supermarkets in China.

Teaching Material Ideas

- Maps, an inflatable globe
- Books – story or picture books are fine, but also bring educational books to supplement your themed units. Art, science, animals, etc. are all great. Remember to choose topics that interest *you*.
- Flashcards
- Puzzles
- Music book
- Home-related materials - play money, maps, history books, a video or book about your country, state or hometown.
- Newspapers or magazines
- DVDs – movies, videos and TV programs are great teaching tools.

Games & Activities

The following is a list of classroom games and activities that encourage learning spoken language. These activities may be a supplement to your topical classes or use them on days when you just can't muster the strength to give a lesson. The students love rivalry, so making the games competitive (especially boys against girls!) is always an excellent way to liven them up.

Telephone

Level: Any level

Divide the class into two teams and line them up. If there's an odd number, one can be the teacher's 'helper'. The teacher or the helper whispers a message to the first person of both group A and group B. The game only starts when both players know the message. Then each player whispers the message to the next player in his group successively until the last player gets the message. The team that can repeat the message correctly first receives a point. Start the game over with the second student of each group becoming the first ones in line.

Hangman
Level: Any Level

Divide the class into two teams. On the blackboard, draw spaces for the number of letters in a word. Have the players guess letters in the word alternating between the teams. If a letter in the word is guessed correctly, the teacher writes it into the correct space. If a letter is guessed which is not in the word, the teacher draws part of the man being hanged. The team which can guess the word first receives a point, then start the game over.

Twenty Questions
Level: Any Level

Using 3X5 file cards, cut and paste a number of articles from a catalogue. On the board, write questions such as: Would I find this in the house? (If not assume it is outside). Does it weigh more than 10 pounds? Does it have wheels? Does it have a motor? Does it make noise? Do you have one? Would you like one? Can you eat it? Can you wear it? Is it used in the summer? (if not, then it is used in winter) Students work in pairs and may answer only YES or NO, and should keep track of the number of questions. You can use many more questions perhaps using words that are new or different.

Word Grab with Songs
Level: Any Level

This is a wonderful activity if you think your class needs waking up a little. Choose a song that the students have or have not heard before. Then pick 10-15 pieces of vocabulary from the song and write them on separate pieces of paper. With lower level groups you may want to pronounce the words with the students first. Stick each word to the board with putty (blue tack). Put the students into 2 teams, each one in a line before the board. Play the song. When the 2 students at the front of their line hear a word in the song that is on the board they must race each other to grab that word from the board (this can get quite violent!). They then go to the back of the line and it's up to the next pair. The team with the most words wins. I don't usually stop the tape so don't choose words that come one after the other. If you want to make it more difficult you can put red herrings up. You can usually play the song a couple of times until they get all the words.

Adverbial Charades
Level: Any Level
Each student is given a card with a familiar adverb on it – i.e. quickly, angrily, loudly. Then the class tells the student to do something so they can guess what adverb is on the card. They can tell the student to do things in pantomime, like drink a bowl of soup, or really do it in class, like open a door or take a book from the teacher.

Who Am I?
Level: Any Level
You can use this with any subject. Write the names of things or famous people on small pieces of paper. Tape one on the forehead of each student. The individual student should not see his or her paper, but the others should. Then, like with 20 questions, only yes or no questions should be asked. Perhaps start with yourself and ask "Am I am man?" If the answer is yes, I can ask again, but if the answer is no, it's the next person's turn. Play until everyone has guessed what he or she is! This can be played with nationalities, countries, household objects, anything and it's a gas, especially for adult students!!

Guess the Object
Level: Any Level
The teacher prepares cutout pictures that are pasted to index cards. One student selects a card and must describe it in English until another student can guess the object. This is very much like "20 Questions" but instead of the challenge being to ask questions, the onus is on the cardholder to verbalize the description. Be careful to select pictures that reflect the vocabulary level of the students. Simple objects, like "baby", "door" or "car" are good for beginners. Later on, more complicated pictures that suggest actions, scenes and relationships could be used.

Simon Says
Level: Easy

This game, which is often played by native-speaker children, is very useful in the ESL classroom. The person chosen as "Simon" stands in front of the classroom and issues commands. The rest of the class only follows these commands if prefixed with the words "Simon says". If someone follows a command not prefixed by "Simon says", he is out of the game. The last person remaining becomes the next "Simon". Some examples of commands are: stand up, sit down, touch your left ear, say "yes".

Crazy Story
Level: Any Level

This is an activity that will make your students speak in class and be creative.
- Ask students to write a word on a piece of paper and tell them not to show anyone. This word should be a verb (or whatever you'd like to review).
- The teacher starts telling a story, then stops and chooses a student.
- That student will continue the story and must use his/her word. This student then chooses the next student to continue the story.
- The last student must end the story.
- After the story is over, the students then try to guess what words each student has written on his/her paper. The student who guesses the most words wins the game.

Taboo
Level: Medium to Difficult

This game is a simplified version of the board game "Taboo". Create several index cards, each with one word in a large font with a circle around it, and underneath 2-4 related words in a smaller font. The goal is for students to get their teammates to guess the circled word. They can say anything they like to try to make them guess, except for the words written on the card. Divide the class into groups of two, and write each group on the board to keep track of points. Pick a team to go first, and have them choose a card. The teams decide who will guess and who will talk. The guesser sits with their back to the board, and the circled word and other taboo words are written on the board. The talker must help their partner guess the circled word without saying it, or any of the other words.

Words Beginning with a Given Letter

Level: Medium to Difficult

The teacher chooses a letter from the alphabet. Then each student must say a word that begins with that letter. If a student repeats a word that has already been said, then he/she is out of the game. The game ends when only one student remains. That student is the winner.

Can You Find What Is Different?

Level: Easy

Ask a volunteer to go out of the classroom. While the student is out of the room, the other students change their sweaters, shoes, coats and so on. Bring the student who went out of the classroom back inside. He/she has to guess the differences (speaking in English, of course.)

Descriptions

Level: Medium

- Write down names of every student in your class on pieces of paper.
- Give the names to students. Try to make two students describe each other.
- Ask them to describe the person whose name is on the paper orally using English words or sentences.

Pictionary

Level: Any Level

- Ask one student to be in front of the class. Give him/her a word that cannot be seen by other students.
- He/she will draw (on the blackboard) a picture expressing the concept of the word.
- The rest of the class has to guess the word.
- The one who drew gets the point if the class can guess the word.

Survivor Spelling Game

Level: Any Level

Use this activity to review vocabulary: Make a list of vocabulary covered in previous lessons. Have students stand. Call out a vocabulary word. The first student begins by saying the word and giving the first letter, the second student the second letter of the word, the third student the third letter, and so on until the word is spelled correctly. If somebody makes a mistake they must sit down and we start from the beginning again until the word is spelled correctly. The last student must then pronounce the word correctly and give a definition in order to stay standing. The student who is left standing is the "survivor" and wins the game.

The Name Game
Level: Easy (Raw beginners)
One student sits in the front of the classroom with his back to the other students. The teacher then points to students in the class and asks, "What's your name?" The student indicated must respond "My name is_____" with either his own name or the name of someone in the class. The student in the front cannot see who is speaking. The teacher says to him, "Is it_____?" and he must say, "Yes, it is" or "No, it isn't". If the student in front is correct, he gets to stay, but if he's wrong, he changes place with the student who fooled him.

Ball of Questions
Level: Any Level
Students stand up in a circle around the teacher. A ball is tossed to a student and the teacher asks a question, e.g.: "Say a color". The student then responds and throws the ball back to the teacher. The teacher then throws the ball to another student and asks another question. For higher levels, you can ask more challenging questions or expect full sentence answers.

Draw the Teacher
Level: Any Level
This game helps to teach children the names of facial parts. Divide the class into two teams. Then draw 2 ovals shapes on the board. Then yell, "Draw the teacher's eyes!" and the two leading students from each team run up and draw your eyes on the oval. Then yell, "Nose!" which is drawn by the next two students. And so it goes. At the end say both images look pretty good and call it a tie. Another variation on this could be for naming parts of animals. The resulting picture would be a monster, i.e. peacock's tail, snake's head, elephant feet, bat's wings, etc.

Martian
Level: Medium to Difficult

Tell your class you are a Martian living inside a human body to study human ways. Ask about anything in the room, using follow up questions: What is this? It's a pen. What's a "pen"? You use it to write. What is "write"? You make words with it on paper. What are "words"?

Getting To Know You
Level: Medium to Difficult

Pair the students up and give them five or six questions that they must ask each other such as: Where were you born? What is your favorite color and why? What did you dream last night? They will then tell about their partner based on the questions answered.

Listening Exercise (Song Puzzle)
Level: Medium to Difficult

For this exercise you will need the lyrics of a song in English. You will need several copies, one for each student. Cut the lines of the song. The students will try to put the song in order. You will play the song as many times as necessary. The student who finishes first is the winner.

The Game of Truth
Level: Medium to Difficult

Make index cards with topics written on them, like: love, jealousy, money, friendship, death, or family. The students take turns selecting a card, and talking a bit about the topic in the card. For example: MONEY: "For me money is very important, but is not the most important thing. It is only a way to reach things. Success is not measured by the money you can get." Allow students to express their feelings even if it is not their turn. Remember the main point of this game is to make students speak!

Story Telling & Memory Game
Level: Any Level

Ask the students (at least 5 to 6) to sit around in a circle. Ask one student to say a sentence in a story form e.g. "Once there was a boy..." The next student must repeat that sentence and add something to it like, "Once there was a boy whose name was John." In this way, the students keep building up a story, as well as remembering what the previous sentences were. Whoever forgets a line is out.

Active Brainstorming
Level: Any Level
Select some vocabulary categories within a theme; for example in a theme of housing/rooms, the subcategories might be things found in a bedroom, a living room, and a kitchen. Group the students and ask them to generate ideas for each subcategory. Set a time limit to keep things paced. .

Divide the chalkboard into sections, one for each subcategory. A student from each group is called up and their team members must shout out ideas that can be put under a subcategory. The team with the most words on the board at the end wins. It is best to change designated writers here and there so that all can get a chance.

Resources

There are loads of great internet resources these days. Several ESL sites have forums where teachers from around the world can share ideas and experiences, offer suggestions and give away lesson plans and games that they've used successfully. I would highly recommend getting involved in a online community like this, and here is a short list of sites I've found helpful.

Dave's ESL Café	eslcafe.com
Teach Abroad China Alliance	teachabroadchina.com
Pete's Powerpoint Station	pppst.com
ESL Teachers Board	eslteachersboard.com
ESL GOLD	eslgold.com
ESL Resource Center	eslsite.com

Chapter 5
The Official Stuff

Signing Your Contract

Signing a contract (承包 chéngbāo) is never an easy task. Chinese business dealings could not be more different from Western ones. Though you may have signed your contract and sent it via email before leaving for China, you will still need to go through the formality of signing a hard copy of your contract with the headmaster. This version will be stamped with the school's official red stamp (very important in China) and you should be given a copy.

Before the contract signing, the school and officials will probably make a huge fuss over you. You might be wooed with big banquets, fancy dinners, and lots of "We're best friends" talk. Take this with a grain of salt. Though it may seem like incredible hospitality to you, the better way to view this is as a Chinese-style initial offer. Really, it's guanxi at work. They want to make you feel as though you are incredibly special and valued as the first step in business negotiations, and so that later you will be obliged to work hard or return the favor. Put away your own sensibilities about loyalty, as this warmth really has nothing to do with you as a person, but should be viewed as an opening proposal toward your contract.

Your contract should be settled and signed within the first few days of your arrival. Make sure you are taken on a tour of the school grounds, facilities and classrooms when you first arrive. Additionally, inspect your living quarters before signing the contract, or get a list of the things included in your accommodation specified in the contract. Make sure that the necessary equipment items (water heaters, showers, internet lines, kitchen) are already installed and functioning.

Here's a short checklist of things you should expect in your accommodation:

- Shower
- Toilet
- Water heater in the shower (preferably electric)
- Sink
- Bed + bedding
- Sofa
- Table or desk
- Computer (if you need one)
- Washing machine & drying line/pole
- Stove/cooker
- Microwave
- Electric kettle
- Refrigerator
- Cabinets and closets for storage
- Secure locks & screens on doors and windows
- Light fixtures or lamps in working condition for each room
- Internet line
- Ground phone line & physical telephone
- Electrical outlets in working condition for each room
- Air conditioning/heating unit
- TV/DVD player

Don't expect your living area to be new or necessarily very clean. If you are cleanly to an anal retentive degree, best of luck living in China! But, the above list is the general standard for all foreign teachers' living quarters.

THE OFFICIAL STUFF

There are some considerations when signing a contract. You may have demands that you must relinquish, and likewise the school may need to offer up more than they initially want to give. Don't be afraid to stand your ground and demand things that are important to you. When bargaining, you can even ask for *more* than you want initially, so you can bargain down to the things you really do want.

Here are some suggestions about what *should* be included in your contract:

- Salary (工钱 gōngqián) (¥4000-8000 is typical for 16-20 hr/wk)
- Date of salary payment each month
- Accommodation provisions outlined
- School's particular work demands – better if the school does not require you to stay in your office during non-teaching periods.
- Days off (at least two for every 5 days worked)
- Night classes – you may wish to request *no* night classes, which might or might not be successful in your particular situation. Teaching night classes is difficult and tiresome, as it often interrupts outside social time.
- Holidays – outline all official school holidays and whether they are paid.
- Airfare reimbursement - With a 9-12 month contract, full round trip reimbursement is common. With a 6-month contract, a one-way ticket is customary. Also outline the dates that reimbursement will be paid.
- Penalty for late/skipped classes – the school will probably list a penalty for tardiness or missed classes. ¥50-100 per hour is okay.
- Outside work – make sure the contract does *not* prohibit you from tutoring or engaging in other outside business work.
- Overtime – The school should pay you at least ¥50-100 overtime for each extra hour of classes beyond your weekly norm. You may want to outline how many hours of overtime you are willing to work.
- Currency exchange – **RMB cannot be exchanged for foreign currency outside China, nor very freely within China**, (except in Hong Kong). With help from your school, you should be able to exchange a certain percentage of your salary from RMB to Dollars or Euro each month.

Chinese business dealings thrive on negotiations, so don't be afraid to bargain for what you want. Driving a hard line will earn you some respect, as long as you are friendly and personable about it. Say your expectations and desired changes clearly and slowly, as you will probably be dealing with a language barrier and an interpreter. Try *not* to be polite in the Western sense, but rather be very straightforward with what you say. This way, you can avoid miscommunication and make your needs known clearly. Again, remember that this style of communication is common in China!

Foreign Expert License

In addition to the Residence Permit placed inside your passport by the PSB, you will also be issued a Foreign Expert License (FEL) (外专家证- **wàiguó zhuānjiā** zhèng), a small, blue booklet containing your photo and personal information. Within the first week or so, a school official should help you procure some passport-sized photos that will be used inside the FEL.

Within two weeks to a month after your arrival, you should get your FEL. If it is not, urge the school to provide it, as this is your official Chinese ID and it is yours to keep as long as you're employed in China. The FEL can also be used to procure discounts at some sightseeing areas (you'll just need to present it and ask if they provide a discount. Some places do, some do not). It's important to carry the license with you when you travel! It will contain your local address written in Chinese, which is useful for times when you must present an address (such as at the post office). Legally, the license should be surrendered back to the school after your term of employment is up. *However*, if you secure another job working in China, the FEL is yours to keep, and will be updated by your next employer, so you should keep it, in that case.

In The Classroom

As a China newbie, you're probably feeling nervous about what to expect in terms of your school – facilities, coworkers, students, or anything else. This section will give you a basic orientation to the types of situations you might run into. Luckily, there is very little variation between schools in China.

Facilities

School facilities are fairly standardized across the country. Usually, the classrooms are much more 'bare bones' than Western schools. Schools are built from concrete materials and the furniture is often uncomfortable, wooden and backless! Floors tend to be made of marble (be careful when wet!) and the bathrooms are usually smelly and stall-less. Depending on the area, classrooms and offices might or might not have air conditioning or heating. Northern areas tend to be outfitted with heating, southern areas with air con, and coastal/eastern areas tend to be without anything. Thus, you will need to adjust your dress accordingly, perhaps bundling heavily during winter months and bringing a fan and water bottles during summer months. Most classrooms and offices *do* have purified water spouts or bottles that provide cool and hot drinking water.

The students usually stay within one regimented schedule, in one classroom, so the teachers rotate rooms, rather than the students. You probably won't have your own classroom to decorate and become comfortable in, so use materials that you can cart between classrooms instead of items that are difficult to carry. Also, don't expect high-tech facilities, such as computers or televisions. Some schools will have a media room, but even those may be out-dated or difficult to use. If you are teaching in a proper university, your facilities could be much more accessible! Your school should, at the very least, have a photocopy room/center where you can make handouts.

If you need video or media facilities, you may try your hand at asking the school to provide them for you. I've had varied success with this, sometimes garnering nothing, other times securing a featureless DVD room, and in one school, each classroom had its own computer and projector (heaven!). It's best to ask politely once, and then ask politely again, and again and again. Put away your sensibilities about polite – in China it's often necessary to ask for something 12 times before you get it! Don't worry, it's simply the result of a heavily bureaucratic social system and cultural norms based on "five thousand years of history". People in China have learned to wait. So will you.

Dress

Dress codes are usually pretty casual. Check with your school beforehand, as there are sometimes safety rules ('No flip-flops' is a common one); but more than likely, whatever you choose to wear will be fine. You'll notice a lot of people wearing the same outfits over and over, and you may find yourself starting to do the same because it's easy and no one minds! During winter in northern areas, you will be bundled under five layers and probably won't leave your long johns (except to shower, hopefully!). A good rule of thumb is to be modest – avoid backless or strapless outfits, short skirts or shorts, or anything that shows excessive amounts of skin. Comfortable shoes and clothing that can take some wear are best. Before leaving, you might want to invest in some 'throw away' plain shirts and pants, as you will inevitably encounter large amounts of grime and chalk on a daily basis!

Schedule – 安排 ānpái

The school will provide you with a paper copy of your weekly schedule at the beginning of each semester. There will probably be changes to the schedule, so go with the flow if a new timetables arrive on your desk or your classes change without notice. Also, the schedule might be difficult to interpret, as it will probably be written all in Chinese, including the names of the classes.

Below is a sample timetable (时刻表 shíkè biǎo) . The days of the week (Mon-Fri) are listed at the top in Chinese: xīngqī yī, xīngqī èr, xīngqī sān, etc. These literally translate as 'weekday 1', 'weekday 2' and so on. The class periods are listed at the left (1-7, 一 七) with a blank period in the middle for lunch. With evening classes, there may be more than seven periods listed.

THE OFFICIAL STUFF

	星期一	星期二	星期三	星期四	星期五
一					
二					
三		口语 08 双外语			
四					
	L	U	N	C	H
五				口语 07 英语	
六					
七					

Sample Teacher's Schedule

Look at the sample class listed for period 3 (三) on Tuesday (星期二). It says 'Oral English' (口语 kǒuyǔ), which is the class you'll teach. Below that, it lists the class information: '08' meaning the class group were freshmen in 2008, and 双外语 meaning that they are Bilingual Foreign Language majors. The class listed at period 5 (五) on Thursday (星期四) is Oral English and the class is 2007 English major (英语 yīngyǔ). You'll need your Foreign Expert Officer or another English teacher to provide your classroom numbers, and hopefully accompany you to your first classes.

Also, you might've noticed that this sample schedule does not actually provide you the *times* of your classes. You'll need to check with the school as to what time each period occurs. Be aware, also, that morning exercises and eye exercises will occur between some class periods, and the lunch and dinner periods will be roughly two hours. Schools usually operate on a split timetable throughout the year, with winter lunches being 2 hours long and summer lunches being closer to 3 hours (for a daytime nap).

It might be helpful to note down on your timetable when those occur, so you can keep track. Also, the school might occasionally change the class period times, so you might find yourself inexplicably ten minutes early or late for a class. Don't worry! It's happened to the best of us, and you'll adjust to the changes easily after awhile.

Strange Occurrences

Morning Exercises & Eye Exercises

Every morning, all Chinese middle and high school students across the country perform calisthenics at the exact same time, a remarkable wonder of communist scheduling. At this time, students are paraded out of their classrooms to blaring, nationalistic music and lined up in rows throughout the school grounds to blithely gyrate and swing around. Additionally, twice a day (once in AM, once in PM), students perform 'eye exercises' during which they do sets of eye massages that are meant to relax the eyes and improve focus. A word to the wise: use these times to practice your Chinese numbers! The exercises usually include a loud, ranting count sequence, which will allow you to hear and understand Chinese numbers. By the end of one term (or maybe just one week), your tones and numbers should be perfect!

Little Red Cap

Some schools use a duty system where, each week, one or two classes are 'on duty'. The on duty classes are responsible for manning the gates and doors, performing chores and generally keeping tabs on the school. On duty students wear red ball caps, for which they have been termed 'Little Red Cap' (小红帽 xiǎo hóng mào). During on duty weeks, you will not be expected to have class with the on duty students. Unfortunately, you probably won't be given a copy of the on duty schedule (TIC!), which means you will likely have weeks where you show up for classes that are not there! It's a good idea to note which students seem to be on duty each Monday morning. If you recognize students, you'll know which classes, if any, you're exempt from that week. Ask the on duty students to consult your schedule to confirm.

Changes and Class Cancellations

There will be other various circumstances for which your classes will be unexpectedly changed or cancelled. Reasons for this vary, from student outings and afternoon lectures to school competitions for singing or fashion and exams. This will be incredibly frustrating at first, but eventually you will get used to the abrupt changes and be thankful for the extra hour of rest (though, perhaps cursing under your breath at having woken up at 8 for a class you don't have to teach)!

Outside Tutoring

Without a doubt, at some time during your teaching career in China, you will be asked to do outside/private tutoring (家教 jiājiào). It's up to you (as long as your contract allows) whether you want to partake in this kind of tutoring, but it *is* a nice, easy way to earn extra money while honing your teaching skills. Furthermore, it's a good way to make friends and contacts in your city, which may benefit you later (guanxi!).

Tutoring generally occurs on the weekends, as students tend to be busy with school from dawn 'till dusk during the week. Tutoring sessions commonly last one or two hours, and it is even better if you can arrange two or three students to take a small supplemental group class with you. During these sessions, you are free to teach whatever and however you wish, but asking the students and parents what their goals or needs are can help you find a good direction to take. Visit the local bookstore (Xinhua Bookstores are everywhere) for an English textbook to use.

Take the chance to assign projects or more stimulating work that you may not be able to do in your larger school classes. You can watch movies, listen to music or do computer-related activities. Taking the students out to do real-life interpreting is a great activity. Not only does this give them a practical chance to use their English, but you can also utilize their language skills for your own purposes! Get your dry cleaning done, go to the bank, buy new bedding, have a pair of trousers hemmed! It's a win-win.

Reasonable pricing for this kind of private tutoring is about ¥50-150[1] per student, per hour. Even in small towns, ¥100/hr is not unreasonable and you will likely get children from more well-off families who attend better schools and have a higher academic performance, making your job easier.

Typically, a tutor should keep a running tab of every date and class hour that has been taught, and the family or student will be billed at the *end* of the entire course (for instance, an entire summer or semester). You may prefer to explain the Western way to your students and their families and insist on billing more often. Be sure to keep a *detailed* calendar of classes you've taught, the students that were present and the topics that you covered.

If you have difficulty obtaining payment from families, create a short bill showing the dates and topics covered next to the amount due for each class, and then the total amount due at the bottom. Send the bills home with the students, having them translate for their parents. This is also a nice way for the students to show off their English skills, and additional proof to the parents that you are doing a satisfactory job. Writing an update letter to the parents once in awhile is also useful for the students to practice translating. Make sure to go over the letter during your tutoring session to make sure they understand and translate correctly *before* sending them home! Also, having the parents sign and return the slip ensures that they will see it.

---

[1] Based on pay scales current at the time of writing. Check around with friends or other foreign teachers to confirm price scales in your area.

Chapter 6
Food, Dining & Going Out
The way you cut your meat reflects the way you live.
— Confucius

The breadth of the Chinese cooking tradition is enormous. Chinese cuisine is one of the most popular foods in the world. Millions of Chinese restaurants exist in almost every country and most people have tried some version of Chinese food at some point. It's no surprise then that food (饭 fàn) is an important part of Chinese life. There's a lot of cultural know-how that goes into enjoying a Chinese meal and people take great pride in eating. In fact, food is such a large part of Chinese culture that "Have you eaten?" (你吃饭了吗? nǐ chīfàn le ma?) is a common Chinese greeting.

This chapter will give you a broad overview of what to expect cuisine-wise. Below you'll find some basic information, cultural rules and dining etiquette, how to survive in a Chinese restaurant (饭店 fàndiàn) and some simple cooking and kitchen tips if you want to try cooking at home.

Chinese Food Basics

The Chinese generally seem to divide foods into four main categories:
1. fàn 饭 = rice
2. miàn (tiáo) 面(条) = noodles
3. tāng 汤 = soup
4. cài 菜 = everything else (vegetables, meats, dishes)

Rice is the staple food in Chinese cooking, which is reflected in the fact that the word for 'rice' in Chinese is also the word for 'food': 饭 fàn. Most meals involve rice, served either stir-fried as a dish or steamed (mǐfàn 米饭) at the end of a meal as filler. Across China, there are about half a dozen different cooking styles, as well as special localized variations beyond that. As different climates in different areas make certain ingredients more accessible and practical, so the variations occur. For instance, the mild, fertile climate of Sichuan Province in the west has yielded a diverse culinary tradition that relies on spicy chile peppers (làjiāo 辣椒), and it is known for its red-hot food, including the famous *hot pot*. Likewise, the cuisine of the dry, cold north relies on wheat and corn for dumplings and noodles, as well as soy products and hearty vegetables like cabbage.

If you ever go out to eat with a Chinese person, they will usually ask, "What do you want to eat? Rice? Noodles...?" much like in the West we say, "Italian? Mexican? Chinese...?". So, knowing the different classes of food is key. A typical Chinese meal will include several dishes (e.g. vegetables, meats, etc.), sometimes a soup, and steamed rice is always eaten at the end to supplement the meal. **Rice** isn't served in formal situations, as it is considered 'cheap filler food' and would imply the host could/would not afford to provide the best things for his guests.

Meat can be... *difficult* in China. We Westerners like our large cuts of lean meat, rarely with bones. When we do eat meat on the bone, it's usually one large bone that can be eaten around. In China, you just can't ignore the bones. A lot of times, it seems like the cooks have just hacked up an entire animal with a chainsaw and stuck the bits into your dish. You have to learn to eat around skin, bones, cartilage, sometimes pieces of feather, *lots* of fat and probably loads of other unidentifiable bits (including dirt, rocks, plastic, and plenty of other unmentionables).

Fish are served whole, with the bones, head, eyes and all. This can be particularly upsetting to Westerners, as we tend to prefer to eat food that doesn't *look like* what it once was. If you can bear it, the fish in China is absolutely divine, though eating it does require some care and work, as the bones are difficult to pick through and easy to swallow by mistake. If you take your time and use your chopsticks to sort out the edible bits from the bones, you should be fine! (If you accidentally get a bone lodged in your throat, you'll probably be prompted to swallow vinegar to soften it, which really does work, horrible as it is).

Bread is gaining popularity in China, so varieties of sweet, sugary bread are usually available in grocery stores. There are also several local types of cookies and other baked goods; however, Chinese homes are almost never equipped with ovens. Historically, ovens were expensive, so the cooking tradition evolved without a need for them. Thus, baking at home is extremely rare. If you wish to bake, you can usually buy a small convection oven locally. **Dessert**, if any is served, tends to be fruit like watermelon or cantaloupe.

Breakfast (早餐 zǎocān) may range from a Western/Continental array (usually only available in large international hotels) to a Chinese meal with hardboiled eggs (鸡蛋 jīdàn), noodles, warm soy milk (豆浆 dòujiāng) and rice porridge/congee (粥 zhōu). Other breakfast fare includes steamed pork buns (包子 bāozi) and fried dough similar to a bland donut (油条 yóutiáo).

China has a huge **beer** (啤酒 píjiǔ) culture and beer is almost always drunk with dishes or at large meals. It's also totally acceptable to imbibe at lunch and you often see large groups of totally drunk men walking out red-faced from a lunchtime meal at 11:30 AM! Red wine (红酒 hóngjiǔ) will be served by request on special occasions (beware, wine-making is not China's strength). For the strong-stomached, there is also Chinese white liquor (白酒 báijiǔ), a potent rice-wine with a slight hint of liquorice.

Lastly, it's worth noting that meals (餐 cān) are eaten early in China. Lunch (中餐 zhōngcān) is almost always taken between 11:30-12:15, while dinner (晚餐 wǎncān) is from 4:30-5:30, and very rarely as late as 6:00. If you wish to dine later than that, the options then change to *very* late-night snack markets or street vendors who set up after dark and go until midnight or so.

Chinese friends may often ask you to dinner without stipulating what time, as it is assumed you will meet at 5:00 to eat.

Dining Culture & The Banquet

Dining in China is a very social activity. Rarely will people eat alone unless it is a very quick lunch or between-work meal. Banquets, which are formal Chinese dinners, are almost never fewer than 8 people, and often upwards of 10. During your time in China, you should get out and experience as much of the food culture as possible, as it is one of the richest culinary traditions on earth and certainly one of the most important aspects of Chinese daily life. Although a Chinese host would never expect a foreigner to know all the etiquette of Chinese dining, if you know and demonstrate some, you will impress and honor your hosts!

Using Chopsticks – 筷子 kuàizi

The Chinese use chopsticks like Westerners use a fork and knife. Rarely are flatware found in restaurants or homes. Since the Chinese cooking tradition has always relied on chopsticks, it doesn't include large pieces of meat or big portions of food that require cutting with a fork and knife.

Chopsticks were being used in China long before Westerners had flatware. Confucius advocated them because he equated knives with aggression. Since Confucian thought still pervades much of Chinese culture, the practice of eating with chopsticks is still prevalent today. Chopsticks are often made of bamboo and, really, the taste of Chinese food simply isn't the same if eaten with steel flatware.

If you do not yet know how to use chopsticks, it's time to learn! It can be difficult to find forks in restaurants and you will be expected to use your chopsticks skillfully. Here are the steps to eating in chopstick heaven:

FOOD, DINING & GOING OUT

○ Place Chopstick A in the crook of your hand, between the base of your thumb and the bone of your pointer finger knuckle. Using the flat tip of your middle finger, apply pressure to the center of the chopstick and hold the chopstick steady at the crook of your thumb. Chopstick A acts as an anchor.

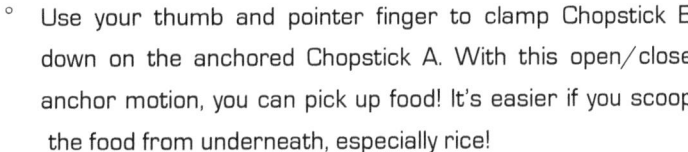

○ Make sure the tips of your thumb and pointer finger are free.
○ Pinch Chopstick B with the free thumb and pointer finger, just as you would hold a pen or pencil.
○ Check that the tips are even at the top and bottom.
○ Use your thumb and pointer finger to clamp Chopstick B down on the anchored Chopstick A. With this open/close anchor motion, you can pick up food! It's easier if you scoop the food from underneath, especially rice!

TIC Quick Chopstick Etiquette
♦ Never leave your chopsticks standing up in a bowl of rice, as this looks similar to the incense sticks on gravestones. Instead, lay them flat across the rim of the bowl or down on the chopstick cradle.
♦ Do not point, gesture or wave with chopsticks in your hand.
♦ Spearing or poking at food with chopsticks is very poor manners, as are using the chopsticks to pull a dish toward you. Use your hands instead.
♦ Do not separate the chopsticks into two hands or try to use them as drumsticks or tongs. Also, if one of the sticks is dirtied, ask for an entirely new pair.
♦ If you are having trouble picking up dampened rice, you may hold your bowl close to your mouth to shovel the rice directly in.

Banquets & Formal Meals

You will likely be asked to attend one or more banquets during your stay. Banquets (宴会 yànhuì) consist of several courses and many different dishes, usually including local specialties. Guests are seated around a large round table with a spinning platter in the middle onto which the food dishes are placed. I am a food lover, so I always want to sample everything!

Dining etiquette is very important at the banquet and face plays a powerful role in the protocol. The guest of honor will be seated at the head of the table, which is the seat facing the door. This is considered the most respectable seat because the guest can see everyone who enters the room and will not be bothered by wait staff entering and exiting. If you are offered this seat, in the tradition of modesty it's best to refuse and offer it back to your host. He will then refuse and insist you sit there.

Drinking and toasting are also very important and there is a lot of face-earning activity that goes into drinking at a Chinese table. A toast should be made to the host and/or the guest of honor before taking the first drink. To show respect, a toaster will drink up the entire cup in one go. If someone offers you a toast and you wish to give them a break, you can stop drinking before they do. To offer 'cheers' in Chinese, say "干杯 gān bēi", which literally means 'dry cup'. Be careful using this phrase because it hints that the two drinkers should bottoms up. If you wish to offer a toast to someone without drinking up, you may suggest that you 'drink a little' (喝一点点 hē yī diǎndiǎn) or 'drink half' (喝一半 hē yíbàn). Refill others' glasses and let someone else refill yours.

If you don't like alcohol or prefer not to get completely drunk, you may ask to drink juice or soda instead. However, since drinking is such an important face-earning social activity, Chinese hosts will often try to coerce their guests into drinking against their will. Ladies will have an easier time with this than men, because drinking is considered a man's chore. If you absolutely do not want to drink alcohol but also don't want to insult the host, the easiest thing to do is to claim an allergy against alcohol and offer a toast with your non-alcoholic beverage instead.

FOOD, DINING & GOING OUT

Eating the Unusual

It's been said that the Chinese will eat anything, and anyone who has partaken in a Chinese meal will know to expect just that. You may be presented with any number of strange, interesting or slightly unappetizing foods and told, with a grin, that it is very tasty (好吃 hǎo chī'). It's better to at least make it seem like you will try every dish, even if it is less-than-appealing. However, it's perfectly acceptable to leave food uneaten in your bowl if you can't muster the gumption to give it a shot. .

Innards

According to folklore, eating a certain animal part will strengthen that part on whoever eats it. So, for example, fish eyes are a delicacy taken to promote better vision, kidneys are eaten to strengthen kidney functions, and chowing on brains will make you smarter.

Stinky Tofu, 1000 Year-Old Eggs & Bird's Nest Soup

Stinky Tofu (臭豆腐 chòu dòufu) is tofu that has been marinated in vegetable brine, fermented and cooked, leaving it with a very sharp aroma (actually, it smells like burning feces). Stinky Tofu is one of those dishes that people either love or hate, and most Chinese people won't think you're strange for disliking it. The stench of Stinky Tofu is so strong that you can usually smell it up to several blocks away, as it is often sold by street vendors.

Thousand Year-Old Eggs (皮蛋 pídàn) are not really old enough to have been served to a Ming Dynasty emperor. They are actually duck eggs that have been preserved in ash and salt for 100 days, giving them a gray color, pungent odor and strong salty flavor.

Bird's Nest Soup (燕窝 yànwō) really is made from a bird's nest, but not the kind of nest built from twigs and leaves. A species of tiny cave-dwelling swallows use their own saliva to create these nests. Men balance on bamboo poles to carefully harvest them from caves. The nests are actually rather bland, but have regained popularity for their supposed health benefits.

Dog and Cat

In the West, people often joke about Asian cultures' penchant for dog and cat meat, however the eating of dog and cat really isn't common in China anymore. That's not to say it isn't done, as some restaurants *will* offer these meats to discerning patrons. However, as pet ownership is on the rise in China, the eating of dog and cat meat is becoming more and more taboo.

Insects and other Atrocities

The Chinese are also known for eating insects, bugs, snakes and a whole host of other strange creatures that Westerners deign to try. In Beijing, there is the famous Dong Hua Men (东花们 dōnghuāmén) night market where throngs of curious people push and shove along a lane filled with tented vendors peddling every imaginable strange food to wide-eyed tourists, from seahorses to grasshoppers and scorpions to silkworms. At this point, even Chinese tourists may shy away, but the food, which is served seasoned and grilled, is generally clean and safe and certainly makes for a good story! Likewise, you can often find snack streets in other cities that sell the same assortment of foods, though none as famous as Dong Hua Men.

Unknowns

On top of the obviously scary foods, there will be plenty of times when a dish arrives that is completely unidentifiable to you. Many laowai have learned that the 'don't ask don't tell' policy works best because you'll end up eating some fantastic foods that you never would have tried had you known their origins beforehand. It's at this time you should remember that you're in China. You came for an adventure, to get away from your home and your comforts, and sometimes it's good to branch out to new things. Be adventurous - you'll have some great stories to tell everyone back home!

In a Restaurant

Like in the West, Chinese restaurants (饭店 fàndiàn) tend to be themed around one particular type of food. Usually, there are the larger, all-purpose restaurants that serve any number of normal Chinese dishes. Then, there are regional specialty restaurants that serve styles of food particular to specific regions within China, like Xinjiang or Sichuan. Beyond that, you will find small shops catering just noodles or dumplings, as well as street-side stands to get breakfast or snacks. Finally, in the late evening, you'll discover the skewer cooks who set up small charcoal cooking stands to barbecue delicious meat and vegetable kebabs (烧烤 shāokǎo) - very popular with laowai and particularly tasty after a night of cheap Chinese beer. There isn't a shortage of variety, as long as you know how to look.

Ordering

The first thing that happens when you arrive in a Chinese restaurant is a warm greeting from any number of servers, cooks, bosses or random hangers-around. In small restaurants, there is often a choice to be seated in a common dining room downstairs or in a private room upstairs. Since Chinese people consider dining to be of utmost importance, getting a private room is very commonplace. Some restaurants will show you a menu (菜单 cài dān), which, unless you're in a touristy area, probably will not have English translations. Often, foods on the menu are grouped by type, so you'll see lists of noodles, vegetables, meats, fish, etc. If you can become adept at noticing certain characters like pork (猪肉 zhūròu) or vegetables (素菜 sùcài), it will help immensely in restaurants.

My personal favorite type of restaurant is that which features a large refrigerator displaying all of the dishes in their raw forms. Here, you can see the food before it's cooked and know more or less what you're getting beforehand. These types of restaurants are very common and inexpensive.

Servers are trained to help patrons decide what they want. You'll notice this is true in many places, not just restaurants. Often, a staff member (服务员 fúwù yuán) will linger over you suggesting items you don't want and impeding upon your decision-making time with their general presence. It's customary for *fuwuyuans* to stand at the table until you decide on your order - Chinese people feel this is good service, while it would be rude to leave customers simply waiting with no advice on what dishes are the best.

As opposed to the West where everyone orders a meal for themselves, in China you eat communally. This means, you'll order several dishes depending on the number of people in your party and everyone will pick and share from them. Most restaurants don't have huge kitchens, so items are often cooked one at a time and served the same way. Dishes will arrive to the table at random intervals, so you'll generally just have to start on whatever comes first. If you wait to start eating until all of your dishes have arrived, half of them will be cold!

Good Manners

Though the Chinese are very formal about certain table etiquettes, they are surprisingly informal about others. People are often loud and rambunctious while dining. In many restaurants, there will be a blaring TV on, as well as loads of other cacophonous sounds emanating from the kitchen and the street. Chinese people don't find it rude to spit bits of inedible food back out onto the table or floor, oftentimes resulting in small piles of half-eaten food strewn around the table. Spilling, dripping and general mess-making are the name of the game. Also, burping, chewing with a wide-open mouth and slurping are ways of showing you enjoy the meal. This may take some getting used to, but by the end of your time in China, you may find your normal table manners mysteriously absent as you slurp and burp along with the best!

If you find yourself in need of something during the meal, it is perfectly acceptable to shout across the room or downstairs to a fuwuyuan or the boss (老板 lǎobǎn), since they probably won't check on you after your meal

FOOD, DINING & GOING OUT

has been served. When you are ready to pay the bill, simply approach the desk or counter and ask for the bill (埋单 máidān). A meal consisting of 3-5 dishes that will feed 2-3 people in an average local Chinese restaurant will run anywhere from ¥20-70, depending on your location.

One note – the chemical taste enhancer, MSG (monosodium glutamate) (味精 wèijīng) is still *very* commonly used in China. Most people refuse to cook without it and there are aisles of MSG bags in every supermarket. Chinese people use MSG the way Westerners use salt and pepper. Basically, embrace the cancer cells! Not really, but you just can't get around it, unfortunately. Luckily, unless you're planning on spending a lifetime in China, you (hopefully) won't eat enough MSG to really cause harm.

TIC Menu Helper - 12 Laowai Favorites

#	Chinese	Pinyin	English
1.	宫保鸡丁	gōngbǎo jīdīng	Kung Pao Chicken
2.	糖醋里脊	tángcù lǐ jǐ	Sweet and Sour Pork
3.	铁板牛肉	tiěbǎn niúròu	Sizzle-plate Beef
4.	青菜	qīngcài	Cabbage-like Green Veggie
	香菇青菜	xiānggū qīngcài	*stir-fried with mushrooms*
5.	茄子	qiézi	Eggplant/aubergine
	红烧	hóngshāo	*in dark sauce*
	铁板	tiěbǎn	*sizzle plate*
6.	酸辣土豆丝	suānlà tǔdòu sī	Hot & Sour Potato Strips
7.	牛肉炒面	niúròu chǎomiàn	Beef Fried Noodles ('chow mein')
8.	华菜炒肉	huācài chǎoròu	Stir-fried Cauliflower/Broccoli
9.	鸡蛋炒饭	jīdàn chǎofàn	Egg fried rice
10.	羊肉串	yángròu chuàn	Spicy mutton skewers
11.	饺子	jiǎozi	Dumplings
	水饺	shuǐjiǎo	*steamed/boiled in soup*
12.	包子	bāozi	Steamed Pork-stuffed Bun
	小笼包	xiǎolóng bāo	*Shanghai stuffed buns*

In the Kitchen

The first thing you'll notice about your kitchen (厨房 chúfáng) is that there is no oven. Baking is extremely atypical in China and ovens are absent from nearly all kitchens. What you *will* have is a sink, a small bit of chopping space and one or two propane fuelled gas burners. Your school will provide you with basic cookware, such as a wok and an electric rice cooker, along with a basic set of dishes and chopsticks. You should also have a large cleaver knife. Luckily, dishes and cookware are very cheap and very easy to find, either in small shops or supermarkets. If your kitchen is lacking in anything, you can easily make a run for supplies.

Some cooking (做饭 zuòfàn) essentials that you'll want to stock up on are rice (米饭 mǐfàn), cooking oil (油脂 yóuzhī) (usually nut or vegetable oil), soy sauce (将由 jiàngyóu), vinegar (醋 cù), and basic seasonings like salt (盐 yán), pepper (椒 jiāo) and sugar (砂糖 shātáng). With these basics, you can easily stir-fry vegetables and meats.

Other things you'll definitely want in your kitchen if they aren't already provided are a chopping board, spatula or serving spoon, corkscrew/bottle opener, scissors, wooden or plastic rice serving spoon and *lots* of bowls. It's also useful to invest in a set of cheap plastic storage containers for leftovers. All of these things are widely available, even in the smallest towns in China.

One great way to get started with Chinese cooking is to invite a colleague or proficient student over for an evening of food and language exchange. Let them teach you the basics of Chinese cooking while practicing English together. They may try to get you to use MSG in your cooking (not recommended), in which case you can just politely decline.

The nice thing about cooking for yourself is that you can avoid some of the less pleasant aspects of Chinese food tradition (like chainsaw meat), and fix yourself Chinese dishes in a way more appropriate to your eating sensibilities. Lots of supermarkets will carry fresh or frozen chicken breasts (something the Chinese don't tend to buy), as well as cuts of leaner pork off the bone. Beef is incredibly rare, but in larger cities, you can find scanty, thin cuts of beef or sometimes ground beef for hamburgers. If not, you can also try out the local meat/vegetable market (kind of like a farmer's market), and ask for specific cuts of meat that you desire.

Dairy products like cheese and butter are *never* used in Chinese cooking, although milk is very easy to come by and cheese can sometimes be procured in larger supermarkets (and it is often just slices of processed cheese). To get the real thing, you will probably have to make your way to a supermarket that stocks imported goods, which will probably also carry pastas, cereals and other Western stuff. You can make simple tomato sauces or pasta dishes out of very few ingredients, and if you've brought along cooking spices (or managed to find them in a supermarket), lots of basic Western dishes are no problem.

Rice cookers are another staple part of Chinese cooking. If you've never used one, they are very easy to operate. Use about one portion of rice to every two portions of water. If you don't have measuring cups, simply add some rice, and then add enough water so that it barely drowns the top of the rice. Plug it in, push down the tab and wait for the ding! Generally, a cup or two of rice takes about 15 or 20 minutes to cook. A rice cooker can also be used to make basic soups if you don't have a pot, and also to steam buns or veggies.

Going to the Market

Commodities Market - 市场 shìchǎng

A commodities market is a large collective of stalls and shops set up in a warehouse or covered area. Commodities markets tend to be the cheapest places to buy things, as the goods are sold wholesale by merchants or farmers. Conversely, you have to bargain fiercely here and usually you have to put up with the dirtiest, most dingy, crowded and unpleasant conditions imaginable. Particularly in vegetable and meat markets, smells can be horrifying, not to mention the extremely unsanitary conditions. Additionally, merchants in these markets tend to be poorer farmers or independent traders, so communication can really become a problem. However, the goods *are* very fresh and cheap, so the quality really beats out shopping in a supermarket. However, the inconvenience of actually *enduring* the commodities market on a regular basis might just be too much for even the most seasoned laowai to handle. Try going with a Chinese friend the first few times to get the hang of it.

Street Shops – 小店 xiǎo diàn

Street shops are usually much more pleasant than commodities markets, although still often un-air conditioned, dirty, musty and cramped. Depending on the shop, it is usually possible to bargain. These places are best if you're shopping for clothing, dried foods (mostly snacks), kitchenware, small household items and the like. Your school will probably have a small shop like this on campus, too.

Supermarket – 超市 chāoshì

Chinese supermarkets are generally quite clean and smart and the set-up is similar enough to Western grocery stores that you won't feel completely out of your element. They are, of course, the most expensive places to shop and they are usually multi-storey buildings with various floors for house wares, clothing, toiletries, dried foods and fresh produce and meats.

Normally, you aren't permitted to carry a purse or bag inside the supermarket, but there are always small, automated cubbies to stow your bags near the entrance. They all work differently, but usually there is a 'vend' button that issues you a ticket and opens the door to your cubby. Place your goods inside and take care to keep the receipt, as you'll need it to reopen the cubby later. To get your things back, either enter the numerals from the ticket into the keypad or scan the bar code with the red laser scanner.

FOOD, DINING & GOING OUT

One of the most difficult things about shopping at the supermarket is the presence of the *fuwuyuans* (waitstaff) who stand idly along the aisles, replenishing shelves and bothering you while you try to shop. The fuwuyuans are taught to give helpful suggestions to shoppers, which essentially means they attack you with an assortment of items you don't want. One good way to combat this is to simply come armed wearing your iPod. Conversely, you could look at the fuwuyuan situation as an opportunity to practice some Chinese, but often they are reluctant to really chat and would rather bombard you with suggested items. You'll learn to keep your head down, ignore the suggestions and hopefully shop in relative peace.

No matter which place you prefer to shop, you'll really end up going to different places for different things. Supermarkets' stocks are varied, which means you might have to go to several different grocery stores to get all the things you want. Larger cities also have Western chain supermarkets, such as the French Carrefour (家乐福 jiālèfú), German Metro (麦德龙 màidélóng and Walmart (沃尔玛 wò'ěrmǎ) . These usually have selections of imported goods like cheese, cereal, salad dressing, etc.

You might want to do a bit of mental preparation before your first shopping trip. Much of the convenience of Western shopping is absent, even in the most upscale supermarkets. They are crowded, busy and often dirtier than you'd hope. These are the conditions that exist, though, and you *will* get used to them eventually. Promise! In the meantime, just try to be patient and take deep breaths.

Specialties

Hot Pot - 火锅 *huǒguō*

When winter comes, you won't want to miss *hot pot*. This is the quintessential Chinese way of combating the incessant, life-sucking cold. Hot pot (literally 'fire pot') is sometimes referred to as 'Chinese fondue', although this name is rather inappropriate, as hot pot is more of a do-it-yourself stew than a dip-and-cook situation. Each table inside a hot pot restaurant is fitted with a hole in the middle and a gas burner underneath, and food is cooked right on the table in a large bowl of delicious broth.

Sichuan-style hot pot is the most common throughout the country, although there are many variations of it and it is said to have originated in the Northern Mongolian flatlands around the time of the Tang Dynasty (600-900 C.E.). With Sichuan hot pot, a large pot of broth, spices, and oil is brought to the table and the burner is lit. You may be given a menu of ingredients to pick from, including all kinds of vegetables, meats, dumplings, noodles and tofu. Other restaurants offer a pick-and-choose style buffet where all of the available ingredients are on display for the choosing. The latter tends to suit laowai well, as we don't have to decipher any menus or end up with anything we don't want, while still getting the chance to venture out and try new things.

Some restaurants offer different kinds of soup, the most common being a hot red soup (麻辣味 málàwèi). Be careful with this one: it can be lethally spicy! Another common soup is a non-spicy, yellow broth reminiscent of chicken soup (清汤 qīng tāng). Additionally, many places do a split pot (鸳鸯 yuān yāng) so you can enjoy both types of broth. Also, some chains now offer special deals, like free beer or other incentives. 川乡楼 (chuān xiāng lóu) is a national chain restaurant offering both the buffet-style ingredients and free beer. One reputable hot pot chain is 小尾羊 (xiǎo wěi yáng), known in English as 'Little Sheep'. Their prices are decent and the food is dependable.

Eating hot pot is always a noisy, crowded and very lively experience. Things get spilled, people yell and scream across tables, strangers toast one another. Basically, the food is truly enjoyed and eaten with a vengeance. Due to the fire under your table and the excessive spiciness of the soups, hot pot is most often enjoyed during the coldest months, as it will warm you inside and out. You'll find these restaurants are at their busiest from November to March between 4:30 and 6:00 PM, when people arrive in large groups, make huge messes and rush out. If you have the time, it's actually nice to linger over hot pot and enjoy every last drop!

Tea House - 茶馆 cháguǎn

Drinking tea is about as compulsory in China as eating rice. At all hours of the day, men with pulled up shirts quaff long drags of tea from big glass bottles, the moistened leaves floating idly amid scalding water. Tea houses are like the coffee houses of China, especially in the southern regions of the country where tea cultivation is prominent. China boasts one of the oldest, most intricate tea cultures in the world and its teas have long been internationally popular. Green tea (绿茶 lǜchá) is without a doubt China's staple tea, although black tea, known in Chinese as *red tea* (红茶 hóngchá), can be procured in China (such as the famous Oolong Tea of Fujian Province - 乌龙茶 wūlóng chá). Restaurants freely serve up green tea as soon as you sit and *everyone* drinks it. Period.

Tea houses are really cool. Oftentimes, they are decorated in dynastic styles, with dark wooden hanging eaves and red lanterns. The ambiance is quiet - you will get your own private room with sofas and a TV set and be provided a menu to choose your tea. There is usually a selection of cheaper teas that come with the set price, while other specialty teas can be purchased at a more expensive cost.

The most beautiful part about visiting the tea house is the massive array of snacks. Fruits, nuts, rice cakes, vegetables, dumplings, fried rice, candies, seeds and tofu are just a few of the possible munchies you might be offered! You can easily spend several hours at the tea house, which is great because it isn't meant to be a rushed affair. Endless bottles of hot water will be brought to refresh your teacup, and the snacks keep coming until you're full to excess. For leisurely, relaxed evenings of dining, conversation and tea, definitely check out the local tea house!

TIC Tea Talk

drink tea	hē chá	喝茶
tea cup	chá bēi	茶杯
tea pot	chá hú	茶壶
tea set	chá jù	茶具
tea leaves	chá yè	茶叶
Green tea	lǜ chá	绿茶
Black tea	hóng chá	红茶
White tea	bái chá	白茶
Jasmine tea	mò lì huā chá	茉莉花茶
Fruit tea	guǒ chá	果茶
Milk tea	nǎi chá	奶茶

Coffee Shop - 咖啡馆 kāfēi guǎn

If you are ever curious about what Chinese people think Western food is like, just pay a visit to one of the many 'Western style coffee shops' that pervade China. Once, when I was sitting in one of these coffee shops with a laowai friend, she and I surmised that the ambiance was much like a large, stale hotel lobby. Oversized booths are paired with marblesque tables amid contrived-but-not-aesthetically-pleasing artsy shapes and sparsely decorative fake hanging plants. Shoddy muzack creates a soundtrack reminiscent of an afternoon shopping at a department store rather than a comfortable cafe.

The supposedly Western style dishes in these restaurants usually reflect the lack of ambiance with their mediocrity - often prepackaged and reheated, bland and very unsavory. The ingredients might both surprise and disgust you - for instance, green peas on pizza or spaghetti covered in barbeque sauce. You may also discover that your first, second and third choices, along with half the items shown on the menu are suspiciously unavailable when a mousy waitress blithely tells you "**méiyǒu**" [没有] - *We don't have it.* To boot, the prices are incredibly steep, the portions are usually small, and the waitstaff are often unhelpful. Though the menus usually have English and photos, expect the dish to look nothing like the picture and taste nothing like it would at home. Basically, if you have a hankering for Western food, I'd go to McDonalds. It's cheaper.

Fast Food - 快餐 kuàicān

There's no doubt about it – China is a fast food nation. KFC was one of the first foreign fast food chains to be introduced into China and it is far and away the most popular among Chinese people. Additionally now, companies like McDonalds, Pizza Hut, Dairy Queen, Starbucks, Haagen Dazs, Outback Steakhouse, Papa Johns Pizza and even Hooters can be found in China. The latter few only have one or two locations in the biggest cities, but KFC and McDonalds are literally everywhere. The setup of these places is pretty similar to that of their Western counterparts, but the menus offer some different items to cater to the Chinese demographic. For instance, McDonalds offers chicken wings and taro pies, while KFC has a huge selection of sandwiches. Both places offer corn salad, but KFC's token biscuits and mashed potatoes are sadly absent from the Chinese menu.

Whether or not you are interested in fast food, it often becomes a regular part of the laowai diet, if for no other reason than to offer some variety and a change from oily, stir-fried dishes. Additionally, no matter how well-adjusted you are to life abroad, there are just some times when you long for something familiar, and you might even find yourself truly appreciating the bells and wreaths and carols at KFC for a bit of Christmas cheer.

Conveniently, most fast food joints do have picture menus and some have English translations, though don't rely on the staff to speak English, because they probably won't. The old 'point and grunt' method usually works pretty well; however, included in Chapter 10: The Laowai Dictionary, are some translations and useful phrases for fast fooding it.

Chapter 7
Cheap Thrills

Most laowai know that the some of the best forms of entertainment in Chinese life come as of a case of beer, a few friends, several packages of preserved chicken feet and an apartment. Occasionally though, the party bug will hit you and you'll find yourself itching to dance or drink with strangers. There are basically three ways to do this in China: Western bars, Chinese bars and KTV (karaoke). Since eating is such a big culture in China, you can also find late-night food markets or roadside stalls to cater to your evening hankerings.

Western bars & pubs - 酒吧 jiǔbā

Western style bars can often be found in larger, more cosmopolitan cities. These bars range from basic beer pubs to music clubs to swanky jazz lounges, depending on where you are. Really though, Chinese people seldom enjoy these types of bars and prefer a rowdier, louder dance environment. Nonetheless, with a bit of effort you can usually find at least *one* Western style bar, even in smaller cities. Sometimes they come disguised as coffee shops with little to offer in the way of ambiance or excitement.

For a complete list of alcoholic beverages and their Chinese translations, refer to Chapter 10: The Laowai Dictionary. This fantastic and utterly useful list is published here with permission from and thanks to John Pasden, who compiled and first published it at his website: sinosplice.com.

Chinese bars & discos - 迪厅 dítīng

The Chinese love noise. They love excitement. And they love crowds. So, it's no surprise that they also love dance clubs. *Every* small town has at least one club and they are usually full of people, even on weeknights. These clubs have one or several long bars, sometimes with poles and girls dancing in skimpy outfits that border on 'strip club'. Flashing lights, disco balls and lasers flare above bar stools, tall tables and posh private booths. And, of course, the dance floor, smaller than you'd expect, tends to be thickly crowded when there is dancing going on. Also, since meals are eaten at early hours in China, partying commences and ends early. You may find yourself good and drunk and on the way home before midnight, having eaten and danced 'till you dropped. On the sadder end of the scale, there is sometimes a noticeable lack of social appropriateness at discos. Case in point would be the admittance of children into dance clubs, bars and KTV halls, which doesn't actually present a legal problem, as there is no minimum drinking age in China anyway.

KTV - 卡拉OK kǎlāOK

We know karaoke by its Japanese name, but in China it's referred to as 'KTV'. In addition to eating, sleeping and spitting, Chinese people *love* to sing. And I do mean love. They will sing on the bus, in the car, in class, at work, alone or with people, along with the TV, during dinner, while cooking, in the middle of McDonalds, while shopping, while riding a motorbike, even while smoking. In China, it doesn't matter whether or not you sing well, the point is that you sing something. So KTV is incredibly popular.

The best way to do KTV is to gather a lot of friends and go in a big group. Try to take along as many foreign friends as you can, or you will end up sitting and listening to very poor renditions of Chinese songs from the 1980s all night. Most KTV clubs do offer English lyrics, though the selections are sometimes atrocious (generally they are better at more expensive places).

KTV is performed in the original Japanese style: privately. You rent an individual room and, since entertainment in China is never had without making a mess, there is the option to buy a lot of booze and other refreshments. You usually need the booze to make KTV into a good time, but it's often monstrously expensive. I always opt to eat dinner and drink a lot of beer beforehand, and then just purchase a few bottles after I arrive at the club. A compulsory fruit plate always comes free of charge, also.

KTV rooms range from completely poshed-out to disgustingly dingy. Sometimes the cheaper KTV halls also moonlight as brothels, but that doesn't make them unsafe and usually isn't a problem if you just want to go and sing. No matter what price-end you go with, the rooms always have sofas, tables, microphones (麦克风 màikèfēng) and a TV or screen to display the song lyrics (歌词 gēcí). You will be charged by the hour (小时 **xiǎoshí**), and there is usually a minimum number of hours you must pay for to start. After that, you are turned loose in the room - use the computer to choose your songs, and sing until you die!

Chapter 8
Laowai Health

China isn't the easiest place to stay healthy (健康 jiànkāng). Poor hygiene conditions, bad air pollution, humidity and the oily diet are all potential health risks. Additionally, the Chinese lifestyle is more taxing and difficult than the Western one. The accumulation of daily physical stresses might result in a health problem or two during your stay. Usually these are minor easily treated conditions; however, if you are in poor health or have a chronic illness, consult a doctor before deciding to come to China. Many Chinese schools will not hire foreign teachers with health conditions, and you might be asked to submit a health certificate from your doctor, as well as undergo a health exam after arriving in China.

Health Exam - 身体检查 shēntī jiǎnchá

Every foreign teacher must face the horror of having a medical exam after arriving in China, or annually if you stay longer than one year. Really, it's not so bad if you know what you're in for. The exam is pretty comprehensive, but it varies according to provincial and local regulations. Your school will arrange this exam for you and should give you ample (read: an evening, TIC!) notice. Be sure you're taken to a large, public hospital and not a creepy back room. The exam includes blood and urine tests and other procedures like hearing, vision, reflex and bone tests and x-ray scans. Women may also have the pleasure of receiving a vaginal exam and/or an ultrasound! Try to make the best of it and treat yourself to an ice cream (or hard liquor) afterwards.

Common Ailments

Intestinal troubles are extremely common, especially for the first few weeks as your body adjusts to a new diet, lifestyle and time zone. Chinese cooking spares no expense with oil, which contributes to loose stool. In fact, many laowai will tell you it's not uncommon to have recurring diarrhea often. Keep hydrated with boiled/purified water. You shouldn't be too worried unless the diarrhea is accompanied by other symptoms, like bloody stool, vomiting or fever. In that case, you should go to a doctor or hospital for treatment.

Respiratory problems are also extremely common because of China's soiled, smoggy air. It's possible you might experience a recurring cough or congestion. Some people find it useful to invest in an industrial face mask for protection from the pollution! Generally speaking, you'll regularly cough up phlegm and blow black grime out of your nose. While there is no way to completely avoid getting sick (病 bìng), there are some general tricks to staying healthy, especially as you adjust in the first few weeks.

TIC Health Tips

- **Stay hydrated.** Drink plenty of purified water and carry a water bottle with you. Drop some tea into your bottle to help the taste. If boiling your own water at home, make sure it stays at a hard boil for 3-5 minutes.
- **Personal hygiene.** Wash your hands and shower regularly. China is grimy and you will be too.
- **Eat clean.** Look for restaurants that appear to be bright and busy. Street food is quite safe, especially if you can watch it being cooked. You might want to avoid pre-cooked food that has been sitting out.
- **Know yourself.** If you aren't sure of your allergies, don't eat questionable things. Shellfish are a hepatitis risk in China.
- **Get enough rest.** Sleep hours are key, especially when recovering from jet lag and culture shock. Allow yourself plenty of time to sleep and don't push yourself, especially in extreme weather.

Getting A Cold - 感冒 gǎnmào

Eventually, you are going to come down with a cold or the flu (流感 liúgǎn) during your stay. As was suggested in the packing section of the book, bring along some over-the-counter remedies from home - things like cough syrup, Nyquil tablets and painkillers. The last thing you want to be doing when you catch a cold is trudging out to the pharmacy shop with your phrasebook to procure cough medicine that tastes like strychnine!

Pharmacy - 药方 yàofáng

Pharmacies are incredibly common in China, with one on nearly every street corner. You can spot them easily because they usually have green signs with a medical cross symbol on them. Going into a pharmacy might feel intimidating at first, but they are usually just small shops with counters and shelves overflowing with boxes of different drugs. Larger shops will carry other medical supplies, such as bandages (绷带 bēngdài), band-aids (创可贴 chuāngkětiē) and the like.

As you might expect, much of what's sold in these shops is herbal, going back to traditional Chinese medicine. These herbal remedies are hard to sort out and good luck finding a Chinese person who can explain them all to you in understandable terms. It's your personal choice whether you buy into or trust traditional Chinese medicine, but I *have* had success trying some traditional cures. For instance, I have frequently used Niúhuáng Xiāoyán Piàn (牛黄消炎片), an anti-inflammatory herbal treatment created from cow gallstones. It's never failed to cure my sore throats! Sounds weird? TIC! Certainly, don't try anything without the advice of a Chinese nurse or doctor and you might need to have a Chinese friend accompany you to translate.

Many drugs that require a prescription in Western countries are sold over-the-counter in China, and pain tablets are easy to get. For instance, antibiotics (康生素 kàngshēng sù) are extremely easy to come by, not to mention cheap. The most commonly sold antibiotic in China is Roxithromycin, a relative of Erythromycin, useful for most basic viruses and illnesses you'll come down with during your stay. However, be aware that taking antibiotics regularly is not recommended without the consultation of a doctor.

It's worth noting that China, being the land of fakes, is one of the leading producers of counterfeit drugs. Make sure you purchase your medicines in a large reputable pharmacy shop (ask friends or colleagues for a recommendation) and avoid sketchy-looking shops or vendors that try to bargain with you over the price. Never buy drugs off the street.

Hospital – 医院 yīyuàn

Frankly speaking, Chinese hospitals do little for soul-comfort. They're streamlined to deal with the masses and inside you will likely see loads of visibly sick people strewn about on waiting room chairs and benches. Visiting a hospital might actually make you feel more ill than you were before you went in! These days, IV drips (点滴 diǎndī) are all the rage in terms of modern Chinese remedies. People will get an IV drip for something as minor as a cold or rash. This system is fairly unpleasant - patients are seated in rows of hard plastic chairs for endless hours on IV drips. Occasionally, patients will also be allowed to take the IVs home and you can spot people walking around town hoisting an IV bag up with an umbrella or stick.

If you come down with a cold/flu or get mildly ill and aren't into the IV remedy, you probably don't need to visit a hospital. However, this presents a problem, as hospitals are really the only places to be seen by a doctor (医生 yīshēng). Private doctors' offices are scarce and mistrusted by most Chinese. That said, the nurses (护士 hùshi) and staff in pharmacy shops, as well as other small medical shops on the street, can be trustworthy with information about the correct drug for minor ailments. If you are teaching in a large school, you may also have access to an on-campus medical center or nurse's office, which are generally very trustworthy and the fees might even be reimbursed or waived for teachers.

The best rule of thumb is to judge your own symptoms and decide on the severity. If you are vomiting (呕吐 ǒutù) and feverish (发烧 fāshāo) for more than 48 hours, it would be very wise to seek medical help. If you simply suffer from a sore throat (喉咙痛 hóulóng tòng) or cough (咳嗽 késòu), you would probably be safe to try your hand at the pharmacy shop. When in doubt, contact your Foreign Expert Officer or an English-speaking colleague or official from your school for medical help.

Oddities

With such a long history and a rich medical tradition, ailments and remedies exist in China that might seem very strange to the average Westerner. For instance, *tui na* (推拿 tuīná) is an anecdotal remedy for extreme heat that involves pinching, rubbing, kneading and rolling the body (especially near joints), sometimes to the point of bruising. This remedy is related to the more well-known acupressure techniques of Oriental medicine. During summertime, people sometimes have bruises on their arms or necks - many Chinese swear that this remedy really does relieve high body temperatures!

During winter, especially in areas that lack good heating and insulation, frostbite (霜害 shuānghài) occurs. Strangely, the temperature does not need to drop below freezing for frostbite to develop. Rather, it is the combination of prolonged and relentlessly low temperatures that causes frostbite. It is especially common in schools where student accommodations lack heating and hot water. Gloves, hats, thermal underwear and protective clothing are essential to keeping yourself warm and healthy during the winter A thick skin is necessary to combat the overwhelming feeling of sadness when you spot your student's hand purple and swollen with frostbite.

Dentists - 牙医 yáyī

China has an abundance of cheap, decent dentists. It's best to check around with friends and colleagues, or even consult a local expat magazine (if there is one) for tips on the best dentists. In large cities, English-speaking dentists are quite reputable and they will usually provide the same services that a Western dentist would, such as a filling (补牙 bǔyá), but for a fraction of the cost. If you need intensive dental or cosmetic work done, that might also be possible (though, again, check for reliability and reputation). Take a Chinese-speaking friend with you to the first consultation so as to check out the procedures and the dentist's language ability.

Sexual Health

Sexually transmitted diseases (性传播疾病 xìng chuánbò jíbìng) are ever more common in China, so if you plan to be sexually active (good luck!), be careful. Prostitution is rampant in many cities, and some hotels do double duty as brothels. Condoms (避孕套 bìyùn tào) are incredibly easy to come by in supermarkets and pharmacy shops, though their quality and reliability are questionable. Durex brand condoms are widely sold, but it might also be handy to bring some from home if you anticipate having sex.

Women's Health

Oral contraceptives (避孕药 bìyùn yào) are also widely available over-the-counter in pharmacy shops. There are two major brands of birth control sold at most pharmacy shops: Marvelon (妈富隆 māfùlóng) and Minulet (敏定偶 mǐndìngǒu). Both are mono-phasic (each pill contains the same dose) combination pills of estrogen and progestin. A one-month supply of either pill should run between ¥15-30, depending on your location. Marvelon is also sold in Canada and is the more reputable of the two.

If you are currently taking a form of oral contraceptive, you might experience some side effects when changing to a new pill. Be sure to check the drug contents of your current pill and try to choose the Chinese counterpart that is most similar to it. Marvelon contains 30 micrograms of ethinyloestradiol (a.k.a. ethinyl estradiol, ethinylestradiol) and 150 micrograms desogestrel. Minulet contains 30 micrograms ethinyloestradiol (a.k.a. ethinyl estradiol, ethinylestradiol) and 75 micrograms gestodene.

When taking oral contraceptives, it is important to understand how your body works and how the pills work. If you have never been on an oral contraceptive before, it is not recommendable to start on one without first consulting a doctor. It is also important to get regular blood pressure checks and to watch out for signs of blood clotting, like leg cramps. As with anything, do your homework. If you aren't sure about switching, check the internet for reviews of the pills before using them or consult your doctor at home before leaving China on what your options might be for an extended prescription of your current contraceptive.

Despite its wide availability, birth control is still frowned upon by many Chinese. Doctors sometimes suggest the use of condoms instead of oral contraceptives. As well, other practices are used to alleviate the risk of pregnancy for Chinese women, such as compulsory surgery after the first child. China's traditional, conservative social norms also help cut down on unwanted pregnancy, as many couples abstain from sex until marriage.

If you decide to quit your birth control use, bear in mind that your body may change afterwards. If you've been on the pill for awhile, you could experience lots of shifts, including an irregular cycle, mood swings, intensified menstrual cramps and other pseudo-illnesses like constipation and nausea. Additionally, the huge geographical change can give your body a major shock. It's not uncommon to have irregular (or even skipped) cycles and other abnormal body behavior. Expect the unexpected during your first few months until you adjust to the new time zone, diet and lifestyle.

OBGYNs and gynecologists are difficult to find and the language barrier makes going to one that much harder, so if you're only staying for one year, you are better off having exams before and after your trip and simply not worrying about it during your stay in China. I always schedule trips to the OBGYN during my annual visit to the U.S. If you become pregnant while in China, you're way out of the league of this book and I wish you the best of luck with that (perhaps you should arrange a phone consultation with your doctor at home as the first course of action).

Chapter 9
Becoming a Travel Junkie

There is no doubt that you will want to get out and explore other parts of the country during your time in China. Luckily, it is a generally cheap and beautiful place to go on holidays (放假 fàngjià). Hotels and transport abound and there is no shortage of interesting sites to see, especially of the historical variety. As well, each region boasts a different type of cuisine and culture, so there are unique places to visit all over the country.

Perhaps the most unfortunate part about traveling (旅行 lǚxíng) in China is that it's not easy. Although the work you put in to get around is entirely worthwhile, it can still be trying. You'll need to remember that standards for transport and lodging are different than what you are used to at home. If you are looking for 4-star hotels, expensive dining or an all-inclusive resort, they are possible to find in China but definitely aren't the norm.

This chapter will take you through the basics of traveling in China, including public transport, where to stay, public holidays and sightseeing. This book doesn't set out to be an all-inclusive travel guide to China, so it is recommended that you invest in a sturdy travel guide that will have information on specific destinations. Although oftentimes fallible, these books do provide a necessary amount of insight into getting around the country.

Public Transport 公共交通 gōnggòng jiāotōng

Trains - 火车 huǒchē

China boasts an extensive train network and even most medium-sized towns have train stations. Depending on where you wish to travel, your journey could take several days and might involve a change of train, as there are several dozen different train lines linking various cities and regions. Many major destinations are now serviced by speedy express trains that zip passengers from city to city overnight in about 8-12 hours.

A nice color map of China's rail network is available from Joho Maps at johomaps.com/as/china/chinarail.html. A quick scan will tell you if there's a line that services your destination and if you'll have to change trains.

Train services ranging from very slow old trains to very fast new ones. The fastest express trains run between major cities, shortening travel time between Shanghai and Beijing, for example, to eight hours overnight. When buying tickets (火车票 huǒchē piào), you should distinguish between slow (慢 màn) and express (快 kuài) trains and the type of seat you desire.

A classification system exists for each type of train line so that passengers can tell how fast the trains will be and what the tickets will cost. Express trains are more expensive than slower ones, but are also cleaner and safer. Train numbers indicate the routes, and the letter shows the train's class.

Letter Classes for Chinese Trains

D = Dong – Bullet train, non-stop super fast.

Z = Zhi – Non-stop. Run only on major routes, e.g. Beijing-Shanghai.

T = Te – Blue trains that stop in the big cities along any route.

K = Kuai – Orange trains that stop at mid-level cities.

N = Nei – Inter-city trains that stop at all important stations along a route.

When in doubt, avoid trains marked "I" or un-lettered routes as they are extremely slow, local trains that stop at every station along a route and, without air conditioning, can be agonizingly hot during the summer.

There are four classes of seating on any Chinese train: hard and soft seats, and hard and soft sleepers. **Hard seats** (硬座 yìngzuò) are as bad, if not worse, than they sound. Usually hard seat cars are over-filled and some passengers are sold standing-room only tickets. These cars are often full of not only people but also insane amounts of luggage, food, plants and sometimes even animals. Air conditioning and heating are non-existent in hard seat cars and often thieves work these areas of trains more heavily, so you should be watchful of your belongings. The upside to getting a hard seat ticket is that they are so cheap as to be virtually free; on the other hand, you get what you pay for. The only reasonable time to take a hard seat would be on a very short journey of a few hours or less.

Soft seats (软座 ruǎnzuò) are generally much more pleasant than hard seats. They tend to be cleaner and sometimes have air conditioning and heating. The seats themselves are usually bigger and more comfortable. As well, standing room tickets generally aren't sold for soft seat cars. On some of the newer express trains, soft seat cars are equipped with hot water dispensers and the bathrooms are kept sparkling clean by attendants who mop them down after each use. If you are on an express train journey of eight hours or less, it is entirely possible to stay the course in a soft seat, as it is much like spending the night on an airplane.

Hard sleepers (硬卧 yìngwò) are not nearly as bad as hard seats, though they are often bare bones and lacking in facilities. Hard sleeper cars contain door-less sleeping compartments, each with six beds. The beds are 'stacked' one on top of the other, bunk bed style, leaving the person on the top bed with a long journey upwards and often relegating the person on the bottom bed to having other people sit on their bed during waking hours. It is possible to specify which bed you prefer when you are purchasing the tickets: top bed (上卧 shàngwò), middle bed (中卧 zhōngwò) or bottom bed (下卧 xiàwò).

Hard sleeper cars are usually the best value, as they tend to be considerably cheaper than soft sleepers but not much more expensive than soft seats, and are completely appropriate for more seasoned or budget travelers who don't mind spending the night in slightly cramped quarters with strangers.

Soft sleepers (软卧 ruǎnwò) are the most expensive and the most superior type of train accommodation available, equivalent to first-class, if Chinese trains had such a thing. Soft sleepers cars have 4-bed private compartments with lockable doors and an overhead luggage stow. The beds tend to be much more comfortable than hard sleepers and some of the newer trains even offer individual flat plasma screen TVs with private headsets at each bed.

While trains do offer **food service**, it tends to be fairly unpleasant and more expensive than one would hope. There are dining cars, but the best way to weather a night on the train is to bring along an assortment of snacks and drinks. Things like nuts, fruits, instant noodles, chips and pastries travel well. Beer is also sold on trains but again, tends to be comparatively expensive, so if you plan to drink, buy your booze before you get on board (and make sure you have a bottle cap opener or corkscrew!).

You can usually buy train tickets on the day of travel at the train station (火车站 huǒchēzhàn) from which you will depart. Depending on how large the station is (Beijing and Shanghai stations are massive and confusing), there will be any number of vending windows with lines of people waiting to purchase tickets. It's best to arrive well in advance (several hours) of the departure time or to buy tickets a day or two before. During peak seasons and holiday periods, tickets sell out almost immediately and can sometimes be impossible to get. In that case, hotels, hostels or travel agencies will be your best bet for booking train tickets (though bear in mind that they will charge an extra fee). If you are traveling in a group, make sure when buying tickets that you are located in the same or a neighboring compartment (in the case of more than 4 people) as your companions.

BECOMING A TRAVEL JUNKIE

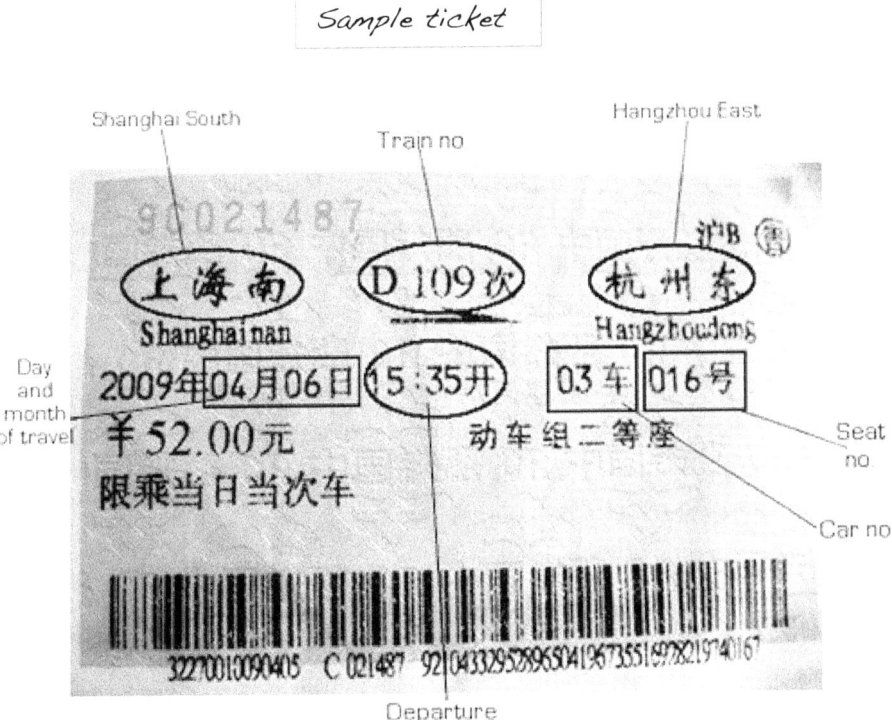
Sample ticket

Large cities have multiple train stations, with each one serving different areas of the country, named for their location within the city: south, north, east or west – 南 nán, 北 běi, 东 dōng, 西 xī. The north train station, for instance, will be named 火车北站 huǒchē běizhàn, etc. You can check train and bus schedules online at huochepiao.com or piaojia.cn. You'll need to be able to type (or cut and paste) the names of your departure and destination cities in Chinese into the text boxes at the top of the page. This will take you to a list of scheduled trains, including the train number, the length of the journey, and available seats listed from left to right (hard seat to soft sleeper) Another site, ipiao.com, has schedules in English.

Buses - 公共汽车 gōnggòngqìchē

Buses, along with hard seat trains, are the cheapest way to travel in China. The advantage to taking buses is that they usually serve more obscure destinations where trains don't necessarily go. In fact, sometimes buses are the only way to get from one place to another. Particularly in rural or less developed areas, buses will be your bread and butter for getting around. Since most Chinese people don't own cars, there is usually a bus that goes almost anywhere you want to get.

The disadvantages to taking buses are that they tend to be slower and less reliable than trains. Also, since buses are the cheaper option, they are often more crowded and dirtier. About half run without air conditioning (空调 kōngtiáo) or heating (暖气 nuǎnqì) so you'll want to ask about those features when you book your ticket.

Like trains, bus tickets can be purchased on the day of the journey from ticket windows at the bus station. If you're in a small town, you can just ask a taxi driver to take you to the bus station (汽车站 qìchēzhàn), but as with train stations, in larger cities there could be between two and four long-distance bus stations, usually named by their situation within the city. You'll need to find out which station your bus goes out of from friends, a taxi driver or your hotel reception.

Planes - 飞机 fēijī

Traveling by air is by far the best way to go in terms of value for experience. Since air travel is the most expensive option, far fewer people take planes. Nonetheless, China lacks nothing in air service options. All provincial capitals and some smaller cities have cookie-cutter airports (飞机场 fēijīchǎng) - most have the same layout and are located outside the city. Chinese airline companies (航空公司 hángkōng gōngsī) are also extremely reliable and safe, clean, quiet and pleasant. Nearly every destination is a 2-4 hour flight and, by international standards, tickets are remarkably cheap.

Airline prices are regulated, meaning that all agencies offer **tickets** [飞机票 fēijī piào] at the same prices, plus their own booking fees. Two very reliable online ticket agencies are E-long (www.elong.net) and C-Trip (english.ctrip.com), which offer phone service and websites in both English and Chinese and boast fairly sophisticated online booking systems. Unfortunately, online booking for domestic flights does not include a printable ticket, which means you are still forced to use paper tickets (TIC!) that can either be delivered (if you live in a city where those agencies have offices), picked up from the agency's office, or picked up at the airport on the day of departure. Check with the agency at the time of booking to find out which options are available to you. It's also possible to simply turn up at the airport and buy tickets on the day of your departure, however this isn't recommended for obvious reasons (but will do in a pinch!).

Chinese air travel is the same as air travel in many other countries. The airports have bilingual English/Chinese service and subtitling on all signage. The only downside to traveling by air is reaching the airports, which are located outside the city center. However, they all have **shuttle buses** [机场大巴 jīchǎng dàbā] that run to and from the city for between ¥15-25. Inquire with your hotel or hostel about where the airport bus departs.

Conversely, if you've just arrived in a strange airport, you can usually find shuttle buses to the city on the ground/arrivals floor – ticket booths are located in small kiosks just beyond the doors of the luggage claim or on the sidewalk outside. Purchase a ticket at the kiosk and then present it to the driver as you board the bus. These buses also tend to make two or three stops going inbound, usually once at the main train station and another at the city's international ticketing agency (likely the point of departure if you're heading *to* the airport).

Very large cities like Shanghai and Beijing now have **metros** [地铁 dìtiě] or train services to and from their airports. You must check with information or maps to be sure, as these cities also have two airports – one for international arrivals and one for domestic arrivals. The brown-line Airport

Express train runs between Dongzhimen Metro Station and Beijing Capital International Airport. In Shanghai, the high-speed Maglev train operates between Pudong International Airport and Longyang Lu (Green Metro Line 2) for a cost of ¥50 one way (discounts offered if you show a plane ticket for travel the same day). In only eight minutes, the Shanghai Maglev rockets you from the airport to the city at a top speed of 430 km/hour – a journey that would take 40 minutes by taxi! Most domestic flights to Shanghai arrive at Hongqiao Airport, which is only served by the traditional shuttle bus, operating between there and People's Square in central Shanghai.

If you miss the bus or need to travel to/from the airport outside of normal shuttle hours (unlikely, since the shuttle buses are scheduled according to the first and last flights of the day), you can opt for a taxi. However, taking a taxi will run you upwards of three times the cost of the shuttle bus and you risk being taken advantage of by sneaky taxi drivers if you are in an unfamiliar city. Make sure that the driver uses the meter and negotiate for any tolls before you get in.

Taxis – 出租车 chūzū chē

Taxis are common and reliable forms of transport throughout China. They can easily be hailed on the street with a simple wave of the hand, or may be ordered to more remote areas by phone. (Find out the number of a taxi service from a local person. You'll need some Chinese to communicate your location to the dispatcher.) Vacant taxis usually have a lit sign in their front windshields alerting passers-by to their availability.

When taking a taxi, make sure that the driver uses the meter (表 biǎo). If he refuses or doesn't have a meter, it probably isn't a legally licensed taxi and you should get out and wait for another one. You can also bargain with taxi drivers for the fare before getting in, which is especially useful when hiring a driver for long distances, the entire day, or for sightseeing to areas that aren't serviced by regular buses. Agree on the fare (票价 piàojià), destinations and tolls (通行费 tōngxíng fèi) before getting in.

In general, taxi drivers are very friendly and interesting people to chat with. They may be curious about your life as a laowai and might also engage you in a string of personal questions (Where are you from? How much money do you make? Are you married? etc). This is a great time to practice your Chinese skills with a rapt and harmless audience.

Where to Stay

You'll essentially have two options for accommodation while traveling in China: hotels and youth hostels. Camping is possible, but uncommon and difficult to arrange. Luckily, domestic tourism is rampant in China, so there is never a shortage of decent, inexpensive hotels to choose from. There is also a fairly sizeable network of youth hostels, mostly located in larger cities or at key tourism destinations.

Hotels – 酒店 *jiudiàn*

As in other parts of the world, Chinese hotels are ranked by the 'star system' and their prices vary accordingly, so that 2-star hotels are cheapest, while 5-star hotels are the most expensive. A fair few Western chains are present in larger cities and generally these occupy the 4 and 5-star hotel slots. Marriot, Crowne Plaza, Four Seasons, Howard Johnson, Hilton, Holiday Inn, Ramada, Ritz Carlton, Sheraton and Westin all operate properties in China. Be aware that chains such as Holiday Inn and Howard Johnson, which tend to be mid-range or moderately priced in North America and Western Europe, are among the most expensive (and consequently, best-quality) hotels in China.

Staff at 4 and 5-star hotels very reliably speak English, which makes them a good bet if you happen to get lost in a big city and need help or directions. Also, these hotels tend to have decent Western-style restaurants, sometimes located on their upper floors and boasting amazing views of the city. These types of hotels are also great places for foreigner-spotting, a favorite pastime of many laowai, especially those of us relegated to living in China's smallest and most rural towns.

Much better value are the moderately priced hotels in the 3-star range. While generally unadorned, these hotels are usually clean and reliable and cost a fraction of their up-market counterparts. They are also consistently everywhere, even in small towns, and often have an attached restaurant.

The English levels of staff in lower starred hotels vary greatly depending upon location. In smaller towns, most staff members do not speak English and you'll need to use your (inevitably budding) Chinese or a phrase book to communicate. 3-star hotels are usually hygienically sound and it also may be possible to bargain for the cost of the room or ask to see the room before committing to your stay. This is particularly recommended if you are in an unfamiliar or remote area.

Hostels - 宿舍 sùshè

Hostels are really a great option in China, even if you aren't a backpacker or youth traveler. Most of the major cities and tourist destinations now have at least one hostel, oftentimes several to choose from. There are a few advantages to staying in hostels. First, you are basically guaranteed to find English-speaking staff members who are generally full of tourist information. Hostels also usually offer free English-language maps and information about the surrounding areas and can help you book tickets or make reservations at onward destinations. They also may have bike rental, food and bar service, lounge areas, TV/movies, laundry facilities and internet access. As well, hostels can be a great haven of Westerners for the tired laowai looking for a slice of home.

Staying in hostels does not necessarily imply sleeping on a bunk bed in a massive room with 15 other people, although dorms are always on offer and are always cheap. Most hostels, though, have smaller dorm rooms with 6 and 4 beds, or private ensuite rooms for higher prices. Additionally, most Chinese hostels are as good if not better than the international youth hostels you'll find in Western countries.

If you aren't already a member of Hostelling International (www.hihostels.com), you can become a member online. You can also join the Chinese branch of Hostelling International, YHA China (www.yhachina.com) by signing up in person at any member hostel. A YHA China membership will get you discounts at hostels around the country and their website provides an online booking function. You can also check other websites like Hostelworld (www.hostelworld.com), which offers user reviews, photos and directions for arrival to the hostel.

Public Holidays - 公休日 gōngxiū rì

There are seven public holidays observed in the People's Republic of China: Western New Year's Day, Chinese New Year's Day, Qing Ming Festival, Labor Day, Dragon Boat Festival, Mid-Autumn Festival and National Day. Though not a guarantee, many schools will offer time off to teachers or special incentives like bonus pay and gifts during these holidays. They are also fantastic opportunities to become familiar with some of the more unique Chinese customs, such as the eating of mooncakes during Mid-Autumn Festival and the boat races that are held for Dragon Boat Festival.

Most Western holidays are not observed in China, even those that are widely celebrated around the world, like Christmas. Whether you are offered free time or days off during these periods will depend largely on the policies of your particular school, but you should assume that you *won't* have an extended period of free time to return home and visit your family during Christmas. However, vacations can be planned during the month-long Spring Festival holiday, which occurs in January/February each year.

Labor Day, May 1 & National Day - Oct 1

劳动节 *láodòng jié* & 国庆节 *guóqìng jié*

The May and October holidays used to be the two annual working breaks, so-called *golden weeks* that offered 3-7 days of vacation. In 2008, the Chinese government changed the official May holiday (Labor Day) to a one-day holiday, and added a one-day holiday for Dragon Boat Festival in an attempt to ease traffic strains.

Nowadays, China's solitary *golden week* occurs around National Day in October, which commemorates the founding of the People's Republic of China on October 1, 1949. Unfortunately, the attempted ease on systems has yet to ease the traffic situation, as copious numbers of workers still go sightseeing or return home to visit family, clogging transportation lines and making travel difficult, even during the 1-day holidays.

You will have vacation time during these holidays, but you'll also be battling millions of tourists for train seats, hotel rooms and space at scenic spots. Book your accommodation as far in advance as possible and use travel agents for bus and train tickets. Since ticket sales for most ground transport options do not commence until one week prior to the holiday and sell out extremely quickly, a better option is to fly, as flights tend not to be booked up but are still relatively cheap. Also, check out off-the-beaten track destinations or areas that might be of less interest to Chinese tourists (read: avoid Hong Kong, Beijing, Shanghai, Yellow Mountain and other major tourist spots).

New Year/Spring Festival – 春节 *chūnjié*

Spring Festival is a month-long celebration that includes Chinese New Year's Eve/Day. This holiday occurs at a different time each year according to the lunar calendar and can be considered your long winter holiday (much like Christmas break in the West). Many Chinese people travel home during this time, some for a few days, others for the entire month. As a teacher, you should be privileged to have the whole month free to travel. You might opt to return home to visit family and friends during this time, or to spend several weeks traveling in China. Unfortunately, the masses of people on the move during those four weeks make travel uncomfortable, busy and chaotic.

Another option is to visit China's neighboring countries. Southeast Asia presents a wide variety of vacation options for the adventurous traveler (be aware that you might need to get visas for certain countries, which sometimes means traveling to the nearest embassy in Shanghai, Beijing or Guangzhou). Japan is also an interesting option; however, many people prefer to escape the unendingly cold winter by vacating to the beaches of Thailand or the Philippines, both of which are reasonable options from China.

Qing Ming, Dragon Boat and Mid-Autumn Festivals

Qing Ming Festival (清明节 qīngmíng jié), celebrated around the beginning of April, has been called many different names and is similar to the Christian All Souls Day. The name means 'clear bright festival' and on this day, Chinese people honor their deceased ancestors by sweeping and cleaning their tombs. Ancient beliefs suggest that the deceased look after family members that are still alive, so many people leave gifts of food or sweets at the graves. Kite-flying is also a common Qing Ming Festival pastime.

Dragon Boat Festival (端午节 duānwǔ jié) is celebrated on the fifth day of the fifth lunar month (usually around early June) when dragon boat (long, narrow paddling boats) races are held. Other traditional activities include eating zòngzi (粽子), a steamed rice ball wrapped in bamboo leaves and sometimes filled with stewed pork, and green bean cakes. In certain areas, you might be able to witness a dragon boat race, and friends and colleagues will definitely offer you homemade zongzi.

Mid-Autumn Festival (中秋节 zhōngqiū jié) is a traditional harvest festival, celebrated on the 15th day of the eighth lunar month (usually mid-to-late September). Held on an evening when the full moon is supposed to be the brightest and clearest of the year, Mid-Autumn Festival is one of the two most important holidays in China (the other being Spring Festival/New Year) It is customarily a family holiday where relatives gather together to admire the moon. Other rituals including the lighting of paper lanterns (a fantastic public lantern festival exists in Hong Kong's Victoria Park for the occasion), the eating of mooncakes (for which there exist many urban myths, much like the distrusted fruit cake in the West), the burning of incense and Fire Dragon Dances, where huge puppets made of lit incense sticks are paraded through the streets (the largest of these is in Hong Kong). Mid-Autumn Festival is one of the most beautiful and interesting Chinese holidays and there is never a shortage of celebrations and gatherings to attend.

Western holidays

As previously mentioned, Western holidays are not widely celebrated by average Chinese people. During **Christmas** (圣诞节 shèngdàn jié), you will find larger cities are decked out with holiday décor and cheer, but the lack of days off and absence of family atmosphere can be difficult for many laowai. Other holidays are lesser known, like Valentine's Day, which many Chinese teens seem very interested in, as well as Halloween.

There are a few ways to combat feelings of loneliness during the holidays. First, ask your school to allow you to organize parties or class projects about the holidays. Use the chance to teach your students about your culture and customs. This exercise will give them new English vocabulary to learn, as well. Have them help you decorate and assign those with better English to accompany you as interpreters on shopping trips (be sure to get school permission for everything). See if the school can offer you a room or area to hold the party and have groups of students assigned to different tasks, such as Christmas tree decoration or Halloween mask-making. I staged two very successful 'English Corner' parties, for which my students were extremely excited to decorate a Christmas tree and make pumpkin masks on Halloween. We even had sparklers at Christmas, which created a fabulously unique cross-cultural exchange of customs!

You could also host a holiday party with other foreigners in your area. Make a potluck dinner with as many home-style recipes as you can manage. Play traditional holiday songs or decorate your apartment with a few Western ornaments, which you'll find in small goods markets or supermarkets.

Try to change up your traditional ideas of holiday customs. For instance, I celebrated Thanksgiving one year with an American friend and two Chinese friends at a hot pot restaurant. We ate and drank for hours, exchanging conversation and cultural dialogue. While the dinner was obviously different from traditional Thanksgiving fare, the spirit was ultimately the same – food, friends and being stuffed to the gills!

Sightseeing - 旅游 lǚyóu

In a country of nearly a billion and a half people and 5,000 years of history, it is truly impossible to see and do everything, even over the space of a year. Here, I'll go through a few of the most famous sites in China – the ones you really shouldn't miss – as well as a few that you might not think of visiting, in case you're in the mood for someplace a little off the beaten track.

Tourism is a huge domestic industry in China. The upshot is that sightseeing spots, even in some of the most remote places in the country, are often busy and crowded. They also tend to be noisy, dirty and hectic with a surplus of cramped vendors selling tawdry gifts at exorbitant prices (who often love to target laowai by shouting hellos or other random English words). A large number of ancient sites have been 'restored', meaning rebuilt for aesthetic purposes. This fact combined with the chaotic atmosphere sometimes makes Chinese sightseeing unsavory to foreigners. However, if you go in without preconceived ideas of peaceful pagodas and natural solace, knowing that China is a burgeoning economy with millions of tourists, you're expectations will be more realistic.

All of that is not to say that there aren't a great many exceptionally beautiful, fascinating places to visit in China. The following two lists will give you an idea of some of the most famous places in China (keep in mind, these will be the busiest) and some lesser thought-of, unusual destinations.

TIC Top 10 Must-visit Places in China

1. **The Great Wall** (长城 chángchéng) – If possible, visit a less-traveled part of the Great Wall. The areas around Beijing are the most accessible spots, including Badaling, Juyongguan and Mutianyu, which are the most crowded, and consequently, the least authentic parts of the Wall. Still near to Beijing but less crowded are Jinshanling and Simatai, where original constructions still exist and facilities are limited – bring water and good hiking shoes.

2. **Beijing** (北京 běijīng) – The Forbidden City (紫禁城 zǐjìnchéng) is best seen during the morning hours before heat and crowds set in. The Summer Palace (颐和园 yíhé yuán) is well worth an afternoon of sightseeing, while the sparse Temple of Heaven (天坛 tiāntán) should not take more than 1-2 hours. A tour guide is more-or-less a waste of money for most of the Beijing sites, as they tend to have (sometimes hilariously botched) English-subtitled signs that explain the site's history and its most important aspects. Among the less famous and more interesting spots in Beijing are Beihai Park, Dazhalan Alley and Yonghegong Lama Temple.

3. **Shanghai** (上海 shànghǎi) – Be sure to take a ride up the lift to the top of the Oriental Pearl Tower (东方明珠塔 dōngfāng míngzhūtǎ), which affords fantastic 360° views of the city (a half-level down from the main viewing area is an open-air concourse). An evening boat ride on the Huangpu River (黄埔江 huángpǔ jiāng) lasts about an hour and the striking sight of the lights on the Bund (外滩 wàitān) and Pudong as you traverse the river are well worth ¥50. Other notable areas of Shanghai: The French Concession, which is good for an afternoon wander; shopping on Nanjing Road, which is best done at night when the neon signs are illuminated; the Longhua Temple and nearby antiques streets, which offer plenty of trinkets for the discerning bargainer. Shanghai's museum and opera house are both located in People's Square, a park that makes for a lovely mid-day pit stop. Also wander over to the immaculate gardens at the Ruijin Hotel and hobnob with diplomats over a cocktail at the Face Bar (located toward the rear of the hotel grounds).

4. **Xi'an** [西安 xī'ān] – Though not the only thing to see in Xi'an, the Terracotta Warrior Army [兵馬俑 bīngmǎyǒng] is certainly the most famous site there. Minibuses or tour groups run to and from the city center to the site, which is located some miles out of town. Xi'an also boasts the impressive Bell and Drum Towers and two pagodas, an ancient city wall and a working mosque, which is open to visitors. For a truly unique experience, go for a wander in the laneways of the Muslim Quarter.

5. **Three Gorges Dam** [长江三峡大坝 chángjiāng sānxiá dà bà] & Yangtze River Cruise [长江巡航 chángjiāng xúnháng] – A cruise down the 3rd longest river in the world is one of China's most spectacular sightseeing options. The Three Gorges, canyon-like ravines located along the Yangtze River in Hubei Province, are among the most impressive natural sights on earth. Many riverboat companies offer three or four-day cruises running between Chongqing and Yichang/Wuhan (both upstream or downstream trips are available). The ships are sufficiently modern, often with cable TV, internet access and several food options. The itineraries include shore stops at interesting sights along the way and are designed to give the best viewings of the Gorges during daylight. The construction of the massive Three Gorges Dam, an energy project, has changed the landscape of the Gorges themselves, but does not hinder cruise liners, which often stop near the dam for picture-taking.

6. **Guilin** [桂林 guìlín] – This small city in Guanxi Province has long been a major sightseeing attraction for domestic and foreign tourists alike. It is located on the banks of the picturesque Li River [漓江 líjiāng], where eerie mountain peaks rise ominously out of the ground on all sides. You can hire a local boatman to give you a private tour up and down the river near Guilin, and while you're there, indulge in traditional spicy local snacks. Also worth checking out are the Reed Flute Caves and the natural archway at Moon Hill.

7. **Lhasa, Tibet** [拉萨 lāsà, 西藏 xīzàng] – The majestic, mysterious culture of alpine Tibet has always fascinated people from around the world. Nowadays, Tibet is much more open to tourists but you still need permits to

THIS IS CHINA

get into Tibet and around the area. Though more difficult for independent travelers, some travel agents will still issue entry permits, or one might be included with your air ticket. Air China runs flights to Lhasa from several cities (the most convenient is Chengdu), or you can take the new train from Beijing. The main sites in Tibet are related to Buddhist history, such as the iconic Potala Palace (布达拉宫 bùdálāgōng), many temples and monasteries, and a handful of other religious sites, such as the Drak Yerpa Caves.

8. **Lijiang Village** (丽江 lìjiāngshì) – A famous UNESCO World Heritage Site located in northwest Yunnan Province, the old town of Lijiang has an 800-year old history of trade. Wander through the traditional pagoda-esque architectural gems of the local Nakhi people and explore the orderly waterways and bridges that make Lijiang so special. Also check out the nearby Jade Water Village (玉水寨 yù shuǐ zhài) and the cultural center dedicated to the Dongba religious people.

9. **Hong Kong** (香港 xiānggǎng)- An entirely separate book would be needed to describe the glitz and grime of fantastic Hong Kong. Now, more than a decade after its re-accession into the People's Republic as a "Special Administrative Region", Hong Kong is flourishing economically and capitalizing on its British influences while rediscovering its traditional Chinese roots. Hong Kong hosts some of the most spectacular cultural events in China (the Mid-Autumn festivities are particularly good), and boasts some of the worlds best shopping and a unique Chinese cultural all its own. Grab dim sum, traditional Hong Kong snacks, in Kowloon, check out the nightlife in the Central district of Hong Kong Island, take the rickety tram to view stunning cityscapes from Victoria Peak, wander through the bird market in Mong Kok – the world is literally your oyster in Hong Kong! One tip – you don't need a visa to enter Hong Kong from abroad, but you will get a passport stamp going between Hong Kong and Mainland China. If you are in China on a single-entry L tourist visa, once you exit to Hong Kong, you'll need a new visa to go back into China. Conversely, it is possible to obtain or extend Mainland Chinese visas via many travel agents in Hong Kong if it is your first stop.

10. **The Silk Road** – This series of ancient trade routes, once used by silk and spice merchants as well as religious nomads, soldiers and traders, runs from Xi'an in Shaanxi Province, east through China and ends up at several points in the Middle East and Mediterranean. The portion that stretches across China is a treasure trove of Buddhist history, Muslim and ethnic minority cultures, artifacts and natural wonders. Explore the mud fort at Jiayuguan (嘉峪关 jiāyùguān), the purported end of the Great Wall, check out the once-ransacked Buddhist caves and glowering sand dunes in Dunhuang (敦煌 dūnhuáng), taste-test wines under grape trellises in China's 'Napa Valley' in the desert oasis of Turfan (吐鲁番 tǔlǔfān), gaze upon the stunning alpine beauty of Tian Shan Lake (天山户 tiān shān hú) near Urumqi (乌鲁木齐 wūlǔmùqí) in the country's northwestern Xinjiang Province, and partake in the chaotic Sunday livestock market in the outermost border town of Kashgar (喀什 kāshí). There are dozens of culinary delights to sample and sights to see, but bear in mind that the Silk Road summers are hot and arid. Bring sunscreen and be prepared to get dusty!

TIC Top 10 Super Cool, Road-Less-Traveled Ideas

1. **Tsingtao Beer Brewery** and local shellfish in Qingdao, Shandong Province
2. **Giant Panda Breeding and Research Centre** in Sichuan Province
3. **Bamboo Forest** at Anji near Huzhou, Zhejiang Province
4. **West Lake** and up market shopping in Hangzhou, Zhejiang Province
5. **Sun Yat Sen's Mausoleum** in Nanjing, Jiangsu Province
6. **Mingsha Dunes** in Dunhuang, Gansu Province
7. **Gambling** and Portuguese wine in Macau
8. **Buddhist Monastery** on Putuoshan Island, Zhejiang Coast near Ningbo
9. **Grassland Horse-trekking** in Inner Mongolia
10. **Tian Shan Lake**'s stunning alpine beauty, Xinjiang Province

TIC Travel Tips & Tricks

- Always carry your passport and your Foreign Expert License (FEL) if you travel outside of your city. Passports are required to check into hotels and hostels and to board airplanes. It's not necessary to show ID for buses or trains.

- Show your FEL at scenic areas and you might be offered a discount.

- Make reservations well in advance of major public holidays like May 1, October 1 and Spring Festival.

- Always try to book tickets and make reservations independently before using a local travel agent, who will charge you booking fees.

- Some larger train and bus stations have English-speaking agents. Look for signs on ticket windows that designate service in English.

- Hotels and hostels often give out free maps and help with bookings.

- Always beware of your belongings in crowded areas like train and bus stations, where pickpockets tend to target foreigners. Also, beware of scams in busy station areas, sometimes involving friendly-seeming foreigners who offer to help you.

- Never follow a tout, salesman or seemingly well-meaning student or stranger from the street, even if they're foreign. Look for alternate transport options before using taxi touts.

- Insist that taxi drivers use their meters. Drivers often try to swindle foreigners by taking them on the longest routes possible, so pay attention to your surroundings or check your location on a map. Bargain for any fees before getting in the taxi and don't pay until all the agreed-upon services have been rendered and you've arrived at your destination.

- Don't be afraid of metro or city bus systems. You can save a bundle by opting for the bus rather than a taxi. City maps usually list bus routes by number. Alternately, hostels and hotels can provide a wealth of info on which buses to take. The fare amount is usually listed on a large sign near the door to the bus (e.g. ¥3), or alternatively you can ask a waiting passenger "duōshao qián?" – How much is it?)

- In unfamiliar areas, take note of your surroundings. Brightly-colored signs strange plant life or unusual architecture can be great clues in case you get lost. Though this practice might sound trite, it can be overwhelming not to be able to read any signs or shop names. I sometimes find myself remembering where to get off the bus as "the stop after that big orange store" rather than by its actual name in Chinese.

- Always take a name card (名片 míngpiàn) from your hotel/hostel, which lists the address, phone number and usually a small map. These are useful in returning later or directing a taxi driver.

- Many signs and names are listed in both Chinese characters and pinyin (the Romanized phonetic spelling of Chinese). You can note down important street names, restaurants you enjoy or places you intend to return to in pinyin, and learn to say them to taxi drivers.

- Try not to make yourself more of a target than you already are. You can never preclude being spotted as a foreigner, but you can prevent being a target of crime by avoiding behaviors that make you vulnerable. Here are a few activities to steer clear of:

    ○ checking your map or guidebook in an obvious or crowded area
    ○ leaving your belongings unattended
    ○ wandering into unfamiliar areas alone at night
    ○ taking unregistered or unmetered taxis
    ○ following touts or other 'sales' people off the street
    ○ engaging in illicit or illegal activities like drug trade & prostitution

And last but most definitely the most important...

Learn to speak some Chinese! It is appalling the number of foreigners in China, some living here for very extended periods, who cannot speak a word more than "Hello" and "beer". Understandably, Chinese is a very difficult language and one most laowai will never fully master. Your efforts though, however minimal, will be greatly appreciated by the Chinese people you come into contact with, and you'll be surprised how quickly your skills improve when you start trying.

You'll also discover how willing Chinese people are to help you out and give you tips on your language skills, plus you'll be able to delve deeper into understanding the local culture, reduce the effects of culture shock and you'll grow and change in ways you never expected. It sounds cheesy, but it's definitely worth it, so... "shìyixià!" – Give it a shot!

This Is China
Laowai Dictionary

老外词典 lǎowài cídiǎn

Chinese is a really, really cool language. And you're going to be living in China, where you'll have the absolute, utmost opportunity to learn and practice it – so long as you give it a chance. If you've never learned any Chinese before, you're probably thinking that it is going to be a really difficult language to master, and you aren't wrong. However, don't get discouraged just yet. There are also a lot of very simple aspects to Chinese that make learning it much easier than other languages, like Russian or even French.

This dictionary is a phrasebook. It is not designed to be a course in Chinese or your ultimate guide to learning the language. You're going to need a sturdy Chinese-English dictionary (I recommend Langenscheidt's *Pocket Dictionary English-Chinese*), possibly a textbook and definitely a good Chinese friend to help you figure out pronunciations and practice speaking. You might use a little bit of your excess salary to hire a regular tutor (one of the Chinese English teachers in your school would be a good place to start), take a friend out to dinner once a week for Chinese practice, or even enlist the help of students in learning and practicing. Your lectures can be a great time to pick up on new words and phrases while you teach, as well. This guide is a helper manual. Herein lie a lot of those mysterious phrases that you can never seem to find in the dictionary or phrasebook. Stuff that's going to help you order take away food and get bus tickets. Real life, laowai stuff.

The dictionary is ordered for you to study and learn, rather than to carry around with you. The idea here is for you to become self-sufficient with your Chinese, rather than rely on a phrasebook or dictionary for everything. So, spend some time studying the phrases in your spare time, or take a few minutes to look through relevant sections before heading out into the world.

The dictionary is arranged topically in sections that mirror Chapters 1-9 of this book. So, all of the phrases that you find throughout the book are located in corresponding chapter-by-chapter sections of the dictionary, with subsections labeled in bold and in the same order that they appear in the book. Included at the end of each dictionary chapter are sets of extra useful phrases and generally helpful words to get you going. While this dictionary definitely does not have it all, hopefully it will bail you out of a sticky situation at some point!

On pinyin...

Pinyin is the Romanized way (Western alphabet) to write Chinese. Each character is accompanied by a phonetic, pinyin spelling to help children and new learners figure out how to pronounce it. Many signs and shops, including road signs around China, have pinyin spellings listed along with the Chinese characters, which is great for we laowai.

Pinyin is really not very complex, but you will need to have the pronunciations explained either by a Chinese friend or an audio recording. There are a limited number of words, which means you can essentially memorize the way that every *initial* (starting letters or sounds) and *final* (ending letters or sounds) is pronounced and, voila! Pronunciation!

One tip is that pinyin is extremely phonetic, meaning that the letters match their phonetic counterparts (much like with Spanish). Dipthongs (two vowel sounds put together) are very common and are pronounced exactly like the two short vowels would sound if combined. For instance, "chao" is pronounced like the English word "chow" and "bei" is pronounced like "bay".

Here is a quick pronunciation helper guide for the initials and finals of pinyin:

LAOWAI DICTIONARY

The Initials of Pinyin

c	- 'ts'	- cong	= 'tsong'
z	- 'dz'	- zai	= 'dzeye'
ch	- 'ch' from the front of your mouth with lips puckered	- chao	= 'chow'
q	- 'ch' from the sides of your mouth with lips smiling	- qin	= 'cheen'
zh	- 'j' from the front of your mouth with lips puckered	- zhao	= 'jaow'
j	- 'j' from the sides of your mouth with lips smiling	- jin	= 'jean'
sh	- 'sh' from the front of your mouth with lips puckered	- shao	= 'shaow'
x	- 'sh' from the sides of your mouth with lips smiling	- xin	= 'sheen'
h	- 'h' with a kick, as if you were clearing your throat	- hen	= 'hun'
r	- 'r' semi-rolled, like a cross between 'j' and 'r'	- ren	= 'zhren'

The Finals of Pinyin

e	- 'uh' said from the very back of your throat		
a	- 'ah' said from the back of your throat with mouth open		
o	- 'ohh' said from the very front of your mouth with lips puckered		
i	- 'ee' said from the front of your mouth with lips smiling		
u	- 'oo' said from the front of your mouth with lips puckered		
ü	- 'euh' said at the front of your mouth with lips puckered and smiling		
ao	- 'ow'	zhao	= 'zhow'
ai	- 'aye'	mai	= 'my'
ang	- 'ahng'	bang	= 'bahng'
an	- 'awn'	dan	= 'dawn'
ei	- 'ay'	bei	= 'bay'
en	- 'uhn'	men	= 'muhn'
ia	- 'yah'	jia	= 'jya'
ie	- 'yeh'	bie	= 'byeh'
iu	- 'eoh'	liu	= 'leoh'
iao	- 'eeow'	miao	= 'meeow' (like a cat's noise)
iong	- 'eeohng'	qiong	= 'cheeohng'
ou	- 'ohw'	dou	= 'dohw' (like 'dough')
uo	- 'whoa'	duo	= 'dwhoa'
ua	- 'wah'	hua	= 'hwah'
uan	- 'wahn'	yuan	= 'ywahn'
uang	- 'wahng'	huang	= 'hwahng'
ui	- 'way'	dui	= 'dway'
un	- 'oon'	sun	= 'soon'
uai	- 'why'	kuai	= 'kwhy'
ue	- 'ooeh'	yue	= 'yooeh'

Tone markers

A very important aspect to learning pinyin is to understand the tone markers. I'll explain the four tones fully in the next section, but for the sake of brevity, I'll discuss the tone markers here. Each word is marked with a line over the corresponding vowel, indicating which tone to use when saying that word.

bēi - 1st tone - the straight flat line over the 'e' indicates this is a first tone.
béi - 2nd tone – the upward slanted line over the 'e', which looks much like an accent marker seen in Romance languages, indicates a second tone.
běi - 3rd tone – the v-shaped line over the 'e' shows this is a third tone.
bèi - 4th tone – the downward slanted line over the 'e' means fourth tone.

On grammar and tones...

As I said, Mandarin is cool. There are no plurals, no verb tenses, no articles. It's a beautifully simple and economical language, accessible enough that even the greenest beginner can start saying a few sentences right away. But, it's also tonal. This means that the intonation you use to say a word can affect its meaning in four different ways, for there are four different tones.

Though the idea of tones might sound daunting at first, they really aren't so difficult. Music, for one, is very tonal and almost everyone can distinguish the difference between the sounds of two different musical notes. To give another example, you might hear the difference between the emphases on the words in these two phrases:

"***Do*** this!"
or
"Do ***this!***"

Here, a speaker simply changes his or her intonation to put the emphasis on either 'do' or 'this'. It's the same with Chinese. It will be easiest to take each tone and break it down individually. Let's look at the earlier example of 'bei' (pronounced like "bay").

bēi - 1ˢᵗ tone – high, flat, even tone, slightly lengthened.

béi - 2nd tone – a rising tone, similar to the way that one asks a question in English. Think about how you would say the phrase, "Really?" That's 2nd tone.

běi - 3rd tone – probably the most difficult of the three, the 3rd tone falls and comes back up, making you dig deep into the depths of your throat. Pretend you're trying to sound manly while saying, "Really?"

bèi - 4th tone – the fun one, the 4th tone is a sharp, quick drop. This sounds like how you'd tell a child "No!", or tell your dog to "Stay!"

You'll also notice that the tone markers reflect the sounds themselves; for instance, the high, even first tone is indicated by a long, flat line, while the rising second tone is indicated by an upward slanting line. These should help to jog your memory of which tone is which and, over time, you won't need the reminder anymore!

Basic Necessities

Pronouns

我	wǒ	I, me
你	nǐ	you
您	nín	you - formal (rare)
他	tā	he, him
她	tā	she, her
它	tā	it

Notice that *tā* is pronounced the same way for "he", "she" and "it". Only the characters differ for each.

Greetings

你好	nǐ hǎo	Hello, hi
你好吗?	nǐ hǎo ma?	How are you?
早上好	zǎoshàng hǎo	Good morning
晚上好	wǎnshàng hǎo	Good evening (greeting)
晚安	wǎn ān	Good night (parting)
再见!	zài jiàn!	Bye!
好见到你.	hǎo jiàndào nǐ.	Nice to see you/meet you.
谢谢!	xièxie!	Thanks!

Plurals

们	men	plural marker

Adding *men* onto pronouns makes them plural. So, *wǒmen* means "we".

我们	wǒmen	we
你们	nǐmen	you all
您们	nínmen	you all (formal)
他们	tāmen	they (men or mixed group)
她们	tāmen	they (group of women)
它们	tāmen	they (group of things)

Possessive Pronouns

的	de	possessive or descriptive particle

Adding *de* onto pronouns makes them possessive. It is also used to make adjectives. So, *wǒmen de* means "our".

我们的	wǒde	my
你们的	nǐde	your
您们的	nínde	your (formal)
他们的	tāde	his
她们的	tāde	hers
它们的	tāde	its
我们的	wǒmen de	our
你们的	nǐmen de	your
您们的	nínmen de	your (formal)
他们的	tāmen de	their (men or mixed group)
她们的	tāmen de	their (group of women)
它们的	tāmen de	their (group of things)

Demonstrative Pronouns

Demonstrative pronouns are "this", "that", "those", etc. Basically the words you would use when you're pointing at something. They're also easy in Chinese.

这个	zhège	this
那个	nàge	that
哪个	nǎge	which

The *ge* on the end of each word is a measure particle that simply indicates a vague "amount of stuff". Many other measure words exist in Chinese to indicate numbers or types of groupings (see section below for more).

Also notice that "that" and "which" have similar pronunciations except for their tones. It's really easy to get mixed up between pointing to something and asking a question about which thing!

Adverbs of Place

Adverbs of place are "here", "there", and "where", "between" etc. These are the words you would use when describing location.

这里	zhèli	(zhè'er)	here
那里	nàli	(nà'er)	there
哪里	nǎli	(nǎ'er)	where

The *li* on the end of each word is a particle that indicates being inside a certain space. The Beijing dialect variants are listed in brackets and are also a commonly used form instead of *li*. Their meanings, however, are the same.

Also notice that, similar to "that" and "which", "there" and "where" have the same pronunciations except for their tones.

Numbers and Counting

One of the first things you'll need to do is learn to count. Not only is counting an obviously useful skill in everyday life, in Chinese it is also a great way to learn and practice tones. The following is a short explanation of the Chinese numbering system, which is fairly simple. I would recommend getting a Chinese friend's help or an audio program that will give you an idea about the sounds and pronunciation.

〇	líng	0
一	yī	1
二	èr	2
三	sān	3
四	sì	4
无	wǔ	5
六	liu	6

七	qī	7
八	bā	8
九	jiǔ	9
十	shí	10

The above are the basic numbers. More complex numbers are formed by combining two or more of the above numbers. For instance, 10 + 1 = 11 and 10 + 2 = 12:

十一	shíyī	11
十二	shí'èr	12

In a similar but confusing manner, multiples of ten are formed by adding the numeral in front of 10. So 2 + 10 = 20 (confused yet?)

二十	èrshí	20
二十一	èrshíyī	21
二十二	èrshí'èr	22
三十	sānshí	30
四十	sìshí	40
五十	wǔshí	50
六十	liùshí	60

Other words are used individually to refer to larger numbers, which probably won't be much use to you beyond the hundreds (or possibly thousands). They are as follows:

百	bǎi	100
千	qiān	1,000
万	wàn	10,000

There are also two numbers that should be noted in addition to the basic 1-10 numerals.

幺 yāo 1

This *yao* is used in place of *yi* when calling out a series of digits, such as those in a phone number or an address. When counting numbers of things or with anything that requires a measure word use *yi*, but when saying your mobile number use *yao*.

两 liǎng 2

Liang is used more commonly than *er* in most cases. For instance, any word or phrase that calls for a measure word calls for *liang* instead of *er*, which is only used for counting sequences, numerals or digits. When discussing numbers of things, especially pairs, always use *liang*. When calling off your phone number or address, use *er*.

Measure Words

When counting numbers of things in Chinese, one must always use a *measure word*, or classifier. These are grammatical words attached to numbers that help specify what type of object is being counted. These words act in a similar way to words like "a *pair* of shoes" in English, except measure words are mandatory in Chinese. There are dozens of these measure words and it can be sometimes be difficult to find the right measure word for the thing being counted. Luckily, there is an easy-to-use, generic catch-all measure word that can be used if you don't know the real one.

个 ge general measure word

Measure words are always attached to either numbers or demonstrative pronouns like "this" and "that". For example:

一个人	yīge rén	one person
这个老外	zhège lǎowài	this foreigner

Measure words can also double as nouns. Take the following example of "cup", which can be use as a noun or as a measure word

杯	bēi	cup

When used as a noun, the word takes on the nominal suffix *zi*:

红色杯子	hóngsè bēizi	red cup

Or *bei* can be used as a measure word to describe cups of something:

三杯咖啡	sān bēi kāfēi	3 cups of coffee

It would be difficult to describe all of the measure words in Chinese, as there are hundreds. Wikipedia has a very coherent list of measure words here: wikipedia.org/wiki/Chinese_measure_word. But remember, when in doubt, you can always use *ge*.

Verbs

Verbs are quite simple in Chinese. They require no conjugation or tenses. To indicate tenses, particles are added onto either the verb itself or the verb phrase. Time phrases such as "today" or "last week" also help clarify tense.

是	shì (sounds like "shr")	to be, is
我是	wǒ shì	I am
你是	nǐ shì	You are
您是	nín shì	You are – formal (rare)
他们是	tāmen shì	They are

Chinese uses a subject-verb-object pattern for most sentence constructions. With this simple grammar pattern, you can combine pronouns and verbs to make basic sentences. For example:

我是老外.	wǒ shì lǎowài.	I'm a foreigner.
我爱你.	wǒ ài nǐ.	I love you.
我们会说中文.	tāmen huì shuō zhōngwén.	They can speak Chinese.

There are a couple of ways to form tenses. For future tenses, simply add the time that the action will occur onto the start of the sentence. For instance: 明天我去上海. <u>míngtiān</u> wǒ qù shànghǎi. <u>Tomorrow</u>, I'm going to Shanghai.

There are two particles indicating past tense. They can either be suffixed onto the verb or attached at the end of the sentence.

了	le	completed action/status marker
过	guò	experienced action marker

Le is used for recently completed actions or to indicate the current status of something. *Guo* designates actions that have previously been experienced (past perfect) or actions that happened in the general, vague past. For example:

他昨天来<u>了</u>.	tā zuótiān lái <u>le</u>.	He came yesterday.
我去<u>过</u>北京.	wǒ qù<u>guo</u> běijīng.	I have been to Beijing.

Creating the negative of a verb is also quite simple. *Bu* is used in most cases as a prefix before the verb to form a negation. There are only a few cases where *mei* is used instead.

不	bù	negativizer, no
没	méi	have not, not

Generally, *mei* is used to indicate "have not done x" or "don't have x", while *bu* is used for just about everything else. For example:

我<u>不</u>是老外.	wǒ <u>bú</u> shì lǎowài.	I'm <u>not</u> a foreigner.

| 他没有书. | tā <u>méi</u> yǒu shū. | He <u>does not have</u> the book. |

It is worth noting that *bu* normally has a 4th tone; however, when it comes before another 4th tone word, its tone changes to 2nd (as in the first example above).

Asking Questions

There are three simple ways to form questions in Chinese:
- use a question particle
- use a yes/no pattern
- use a question word.

There is one question particle, *ma*, which is attached at the end of a declarative sentence to form a question. For example:

| 你是老外吗? | nǐ shì lǎowài <u>ma</u>? | Are you a foreigner? |
| 他们会说中文吗? | tāmen huì shuō zhōngwén <u>ma</u>? | Can they speak Chinese? |

Ma works the same way every time and can be amended to any declarative sentence to change it into a question.

Yes/no questions can also be created using the negative/positive of a verb or adjective in the following pattern: *shì bú shì* = is or isn't

| 你是不是老外? | nǐ <u>shì bú shì</u> lǎowài? | Are you a foreigner or not? |
| 他会不会说中文? | tā <u>huì bú huì</u> shuō zhōngwén? | Can he speak Chinese or not? |

The same as in English, in Chinese, you can use question words to form interrogatories. The following are useful question words:

谁	shéi	who
什么	shénme	what
什么时候	shénme shíhou	when

哪儿/哪里	nǎr/nǎli	where
为什么	wèi shénme	why
哪个	nǎge	which (singular)
哪些	nǎxiē	which (plural)
怎么	zěnme	how
多少	duōshao	how much/many
几(个)	jǐ(ge)	how many (under 10, use measure word)
干吗	gànma	What's going on?

For example:

他是谁?	tā shì <u>shéi</u>?	Who is he?
这是什么?	zhè shì <u>shénme</u>?	What is this?
我们什么时候去?	wǒmen <u>shénme shíhou</u> qù?	When are we going?
学校在哪里?	xuéxiào zài <u>nǎli</u>?	Where is the school?
你为什么悲伤?	nǐ <u>wèi shénme</u> bēishāng?	Why are you sad?
哪个是你的?	<u>nǎge</u> shì nǐde?	Which one is yours?
X怎么拼?	X <u>zěnme</u> pīn?	How do you spell X?
这个多少钱?	zhège <u>duōshao</u> qián?	How much does this cost?
他们有几个书?	tāmen yǒu <u>jǐge</u> shū?	How many books do they have?

Answering questions is generally fairly easy. Nine times out of ten, you can simply replace the question word with the answer. Take this example:

他是谁?	tā shì <u>shéi</u>?	Who is he?

Here, we will replace the word 'shéi' (who) with the answer to the question, leaving the rest of the sentence as is. So:

他是<u>我的爸爸</u>.	tā shì <u>wǒde bàba</u>.	He is my father.

Here are a few more examples to get you started.

这是<u>什么</u>?	zhè shì <u>shénme</u>?	<u>What</u> is this?

这是<u>牛肉</u>.	zhè shì <u>niǔ ròu</u>.	This is <u>beef</u>.
我们<u>什么时候</u>去	wǒmen <u>shénme shíhòu</u> qù?	<u>When</u> are we going?
我们<u>明天</u>去.	wǒmen <u>míngtiān</u> qù.	We are going <u>tomorrow</u>.
学校在<u>哪里</u>?	xuéxiào zài <u>nǎli</u>?	<u>Where</u> is the school?
学校在<u>上海</u>.	xuéxiào zài <u>shànghǎi</u>.	The school is in <u>Shanghai</u>.

Finally, it is important to note that Chinese contains no articles (a, an, the) and makes very little use of helping verbs (He <u>is</u> going to China). When in doubt, make the sentence as simple as you can. It will probably be pretty difficult to get rid of those pesky extra words that we're so fond of in English, but just try to simplify you'll usually be fine!

Keys to the Middle Kingdom

Though I hope this dictionary will be useful to you in your everyday life, it is understandable that finding the words you need from a phrasebook at the moment you need them sometimes proves troublesome. So, here I'll outline a few key phrases and questions that you are sure to use at some point.

X 在哪里 (哪儿)?	X zài nǎli (nǎr)?	Where is X?

The phrase in parenthesis is Beijing Hua, the dialect that is used throughout China's northeast. It is really up to you which accent you use in Chinese, so I'm giving you both the standard pronunciation and the dialect here.

我听不懂.	wǒ tīng bù dǒng.	I don't understand.
对不起!	dǔi bù qǐ!	I'm sorry/excuse me!
我叫 X.	wǒ jiào X.	My name is X.
我是美国人.	wǒ shì měiguó rén.	I'm American
英国	yīngguó	England
爱尔兰	ai'ěrlán	Ireland
苏格兰	sūgélán	Scotland
加拿大	jiā'nádà	Canada
澳大利亚	àodàlìyà	Australia
新西兰	xīnxīlán	New Zealand
南非	nánfēi	South Africa

Any country name can be inserted into the above sentence to indicate nationality. The word *ren* simply means 'person' and, when added onto a country name, creates nationality. So, *měiguó* means "America" but *měiguó rén* means "American person" or "American".

没关系.	méi guānxī.	Don't worry about it.
没有问题.	méiyǒu wèntǐ.	No problem.
请说慢一点.	qǐng shuō màn yī diǎn.	Please speak slowly.
我[不]知道.	wǒ (bù) zhīdào.	I (don't) know.

厕所间在哪里?	cèsuǒ jiān zài nǎli (nǎr)?	Where is the bathroom?
两瓶啤酒.	<u>liǎng</u> píng píjiǔ.	<u>Two</u> bottles of beer.
我要这个.	wǒ yào zhège.	I want this.
买单.	mǎidān.	I'll pay the bill now.
带走 / 包.	dài zòu/bāo.	To go/take away.
请帮我.	qíng bāng wǒ.	Please help me.
医院在哪里?	yīyuàn zài nǎli (nǎr)?	Where is the hospital?
有人说英文吗?	yǒu rén shuō yīngwén ma?	Does anyone speak English?
太 X 了!	tài X le! (xiǎo, dà, etc)	It's too X! (big, small, etc)
太多了.	tài duō le!	I'm (he/she's) drunk! (slang)

Introduction & Chapter 1: The Compulsory Stuff

老外	lǎowài	foreigner
普通话	pǔtōnghuà	Mandarin Chinese
人民币	rénmín bì	Renminbi (currency)
北	běi	north
南	nán	south
长江	chángjiāng	Yangtze River
关系	guānxi	relationships, connections, social capital
面子	miànzi	face, reputation
脸	liǎn	face
厕所	cèsuǒ	bathroom
礼物	lǐwù	gift
排队	páiduì	line, queue

Chapter 2: Before You Go

护照	hùzhào	passport
签证	qiānzhèng	visa
迁居移民	qiānjū yímín	immigration

Extra Useful Phrases

这是我的护照	zhè shì wǒde hùzhào.	Here is my passport.
从…来	cóng X lái	from X come
到…去	dào X qù	to X go
从美国来	cóng měiguó lái	come from America
到中国去	dào zhōngguó qù	go to China

Chapter 3: Arrival & Daily Life

银行	**yínháng**	**bank**
银行帐户	yínháng zhànghù	bank account
提款	tíkuǎn	withdraw
存钱	cúnqián	deposit/lodge money
存簿	cúnbù	account passbook
提款机	tíkuǎn jī	ATM
信用卡	xìnyòngkǎ	credit card
手机	**shǒujī**	**mobile phone**
加费	jiā fèi	top up/add money
你 付/ 加都 少?	nǐ fù/ jiā dōushǎo?	How much do you want to pay?
电脑	**diànnǎo**	**computer**
网	wǎng	internet
网吧	wǎngbā	internet café
公寓	**gōngyù**	**apartment**
衣物	yīwù	laundry
洗衣机	xǐyī jī	washing machine
买东西	**mǎi dōngxī**	**shopping**
不要. 谢谢	bú yào, xièxie.	I don't want it, thanks.
名片	**míng piàn**	**business/name card**
按摩院	**ànmó yuàn**	**massage parlor**
轻一点	qīng yī diǎn	Please massage more lightly.
理发店	**lǐfà diàn**	**hair salon**
洗头发	xǐ tóufa	shampoo, wash hair
剪头发	jiǎn tóufa	hair cut
染色	rǎnsè	dye, coloring

THIS IS CHINA

邮电局	yóudiàn jú	post office
邮筒	yóutǒng	post box
寄	jì	to send
地质	dìzhǐ	address
包裹	bāoguǒ	package
信	xìn	letter

Extra Useful Phrases

储蓄帐户	chǔxù zhànghù	savings account
我想要存钱。	wǒ xiǎngyào cúnqián.	I would like to make a deposit.

手机号码	shǒujī hàomǎ	mobile number
喂	wèi?	Hello? (phone)
电话	diánhuà	telephone
电话号码	diánhuà hàomǎ	telephone number
打字	dǎ zì	to type
多少钱?	duōshao qián?	How much is it?
快	kuài	slang for Chinese cash
元	yuán	Chinese RMB
快钱	kuài qián	piece of money, note
几快钱?	jǐ kuài qián?	How many RMB?
三快钱.	sān kuài qián.	Three RMB.

穿衣服	chuān yīfu	to wear/put on/try on
号码	hàomǎ	size, number
大号	dá hào	large
中号	zhōng hào	medium
小号	xiǎo hào	small

邮票	yóupiào	stamps
我要寄一个_____.	wǒ yào jì yīge X.	I want to send one X.
道美国	dào měiguó	to America

Chapter 4: On Being an FT

教英语	**jiāo yīngyǔ**	**teach English**
老师	lǎoshī	teacher
外教	wàijiào	foreign teacher
教室	jiàoshì	classroom
学生	xuésheng	student
课	kè	course, subject, lesson
说	shuō	speak, say
学校	xuéxiào	school
办公室	bàn'gōng shì	office
班	bān	class (group of students)
书	shū	book
考试	**kǎoshì**	**exam, test**
考分	kǎofēn	grade, mark

Extra Useful Phrases

上课	shàngkè	start class, attend class
下课	xiàkè	class dismissed, class is over
及格	jígé	to pass (a class, test)
不及格	bù jígé	to fail (a class, test)
读书	dúshū	read, study
听!	tīng!	Listen!

Chapter 5: The Official Stuff

承包	**chéngbāo**	**contract**
工钱	gōngqián	salary
外国专家证	wàiguó zhuānjiā zhèng	Foreign Expert's Certificate
安排	**ānpái**	**schedule**
时刻表	shíkè **biǎo**	timetable
星期一	xīngqī	week
星期一	xīngqī yī	Monday
星期二	xīngqī èr	Tuesday
星期三	xīngqī sān	Wednesday
星期四	xīngqī sì	Thursday
星期无	xīngqī wǔ	Friday
星期六	xīngqī liu	Saturday
星期日	xīngqī rì	Sunday
口语	kǒuyǔ	oral/spoken language
英语	yīngyǔ	English
小红帽	**xiǎo** hóng mào	"Little Red Cap", on duty
家教	jiājiào	tutor, teach at home

Extra Useful Phrases

号	hào	date, number
月	yuè	month
一月	yī yuè	January (month 1)
二月	èr yuè	February (month 2)
三月	sān yuè	March (month 3)

The months are named according to their number on the calendar + the word "month".

几月几号?	jī yuè jī hào?	
		What's the date? (which month, which day)
七月二十八号	qīyuè èrshíbā hào	July 28th

Chapter 6: Food, Dining & Going Out

饭	fàn	rice, food
吃[饭]	chī (fàn)	to eat
你吃饭了吗?	nǐ chīfàn le ma?	Have you eaten? (greeting)
面	miàn	noodles
汤	tāng	soup
菜	cài	dish
米饭	mǐfàn	boiled rice
辣椒	làjiāo	hot pepper
早餐	zǎocān	breakfast
鸡蛋	jīdàn	chicken egg
豆浆	dòujiāng	soy milk
粥	zhōu	porridge/congee
包子	bāozi	steamed buns
油条	yóutiáo	fried breakfast dough
啤酒	píjiǔ	beer
红酒	hóngjiǔ	red wine
白酒	bái jiǔ	Chinese rice wine
餐	cān	meal
中餐	zhōngcān	lunch
晚餐	wǎncān	dinner
宴会	yànhuì	banquet
筷子	kuàizi	chopsticks
干杯!	gānbēi!	Cheers/Bottoms up!
喝一点点	hē yī diǎndiǎn	drink a little
喝一半	hē yíbàn	drink half
好吃	hǎo chī	tasty
臭豆腐	chòu dòufu	Stinky Tofu

皮蛋	pídàn	Thousand Year-Old Eggs
燕窝	yànwō	Bird's Nest Soup
东花们	dōnghuāmén	Donghuamen Night Market
饭店	**fàndiàn**	**restaurant**
烧烤	shāokǎo	barbeque
菜单	cài dān	menu
猪肉	zhūròu	pork
素菜	sùcài	vegetable
服务员	fúwù yuán	waitperson/server
老板	**lǎobǎn**	boss, owner
埋单	máidān	bill, check
味精	wèijīng	MSG, monosodium glutamate
厨房	**chúfáng**	**kitchen**
做饭	zuòfàn	to cook
米饭	mǐfàn	white rice
油脂	yóuzhī	cooking oil
将由	jiàngyóu	soy sauce
醋	cù	vinegar
盐	yán	salt
椒	jiāo	pepper
砂糖	shātáng	sugar
市场	**shìchǎng**	**market**
小店	xiǎo diàn	small shop
超市	chāoshì	supermarket
家乐福	jiālèfú	Carrefour
麦德龙	màidélóng	Metro
火锅	**huǒguō**	**hot pot**
汤	tāng	broth/soup
麻辣味	málàwèi	spicy broth/soup
清汤	qīng tāng	non-spicy broth/soup

鸳鸯	yuān yāng	split pot
川乡楼	chuān xiāng lóu	Chuan Xiang Lou Hot Pot
小尾羊	xiǎo wěi yáng	Little Sheep Hot Pot

茶	**chá**	**tea**
茶馆	cháguǎn	teahouse
红茶	hóngchá	black tea
乌龙茶	wūlóng chá	Oolong Tea
绿茶	lǜ chá	Green tea
白茶	bái chá	White tea
茉莉花茶	mò lì huā chá	Jasmine tea
果茶	guǒ chá	Fruit tea
奶茶	nǎi chá	Milk tea
喝茶	hē chá	drink tea
茶杯	chá bēi	tea cup
茶壶	chá hú	tea pot
茶具	chá jù	tea set
茶叶	chá yè	tea leaves

咖啡	**kāfēi**	**coffee**
咖啡馆	kāfēi guǎn	coffeehouse
没有	méiyǒu	don't have, there aren't any

快餐	**kuài cān**	**fast food**
份	fèn	portion/order
套餐	tàocān	set/combo meal
号	hào	number (as in "yī hào" – "number one")
小/中/大 的	xiǎo/zhōng/dà de	small, medium, large size
饮料	yǐnliào	beverage/drink
薯条	shǔtiáo	french fries
汉堡包	hànbǎobāo	hamburger
比萨	bǐsà	pizza
鸡米华	jīmǐhuá	popcorn chicken

玉米杯	yùmǐ bēi	corn cup
沙拉	shālā	salad
冰淇淋	bīngqílín	ice cream
巧克力	qiǎokèlì	chocolate
奶昔	nǎi xī	milkshake

Extra Useful Phrases

抄	chǎo de	stir-fried
炒肉	chǎoròu	stir-fried with mince pork
抄饭	chǎofàn	fried rice
炒面	chǎomiàn	fried noodles
牛肉	niúròu	beef
羊肉	yángròu	mutton/lamb
鱼	yǔ	fish
辣的	làde	spicy
辣椒	làjiāo	hot peppers
饼	**bǐng**	round, flat cake / cookie / pastry
有营养	**yǒu yíngyǎng**	nutritious
好吃	hǎochī	tasty

Foreign Brands

雪碧	xuě bì	Sprite
芬达	fēn dá	Fanta
可口可乐	(kě kǒu) kě lè	(Coke) cola
百事可乐	(bǎi shì) kě lè	(Pepsi) cola
DQ冰淇淋	DQbīngqílín	DQ/Dairy Queen
肯德基	kěndéjī	KFC
美国猫头鹰餐厅	měiguó māotóuyīng cāntīng	Hooters
麦当劳	màidāngláo	McDonald's
澳拜客牛排店	àobàikè niúpáidiàn	Outback Steakhouse
棒约翰比萨	bàngyuēhàn bǐsà	Papa John's Pizza
必胜客	bìshèngkè	Pizza Hut
星巴克	xīngbākè	Starbucks

McDonald's Menu

汉堡包	hànbǎobāo	Hamburger
吉士汉堡包	jíshì hànbǎo	Cheeseburger
双层汉堡	shuāngcéng hànbǎo	Double Hamburger
双层吉士汉堡包	shuāngcéng jíshì hànbǎo	Double Cheeseburger
巨无霸	jùwúbà	Big Mac
麦辣鸡腿汉堡	màilà jītuǐ **hànbǎo**	Spicy Chicken Sandwich
特级板烧鸡腿汉堡	tèjíbǎn shāo jītuǐ hànbǎo	Grilled Chicken Sandwich
麦香鱼	mài xiāng yú	Filet-O-Fish
麦乐鸡	mài lè jī	Chicken McNuggets

Chapter 7: Cheap Thrills

酒吧	jiǔbā	bar
迪厅	dítīng	disco, dance club
卡拉OK	**kǎlāOK**	**karaoke, KTV**
麦克风	màikèfēng	microphone
歌词	gēcí	song lyrics
[一个]小时	[yīge] xiǎoshí	[one] hour

Extra Useful Phrases

喝酒	hējiǔ	drink alcohol, go drinking
一瓶啤酒	yīpíng píjiǔ	one bottle of beer
跳舞	tiàowǔ	dance
烟	yān	cigarettes
吸烟	xīyān	smoke
衣帽间	yīmàojiān	coatroom
存衣服	cùn yīfu	check the coats
服务费	fúwù fèi	cover charge, entry fee
冰的	bīngde	cold, iced
加冰快	jīa bīngkuài	with ice, on the rocks
唱歌	chànggē	sing (songs)
有没有英语歌?	yǒu méi yǒu yīngyǔ gē?	Do you have English songs?
中文	zhōngwén	Chinese
日语	rìyǔ	Japanese
宜良	yīnliàng	sound volume
响一点	xiǎng yīdiǎn	turn it up (volume)
静一点	jìng yīdiǎn	turn it down (volume)
单间	dānjiān	private room

The Cocktail & Alcohol list

Absolut	瑞典伏特加	ruì diǎn fú tè jiā
Angel's Kiss	天使之吻	tiān shǐ zhī wěn
Asahi	朝日	zhāo rì
B-52	轰炸机	hōng zhà jī
Bacardi	白家得	bái jiā dé
Bailey's	百利甜酒	bǎi lì tián jiǔ
Beck's	贝克	bèi kè
Beefeater's	必发达金	bì fā dá jīn
beer	啤酒	píjiǔ
Black Russian	黑色俄罗斯	hēi sè é luó sī
Bloody Mary	血腥玛丽	xuè xīng mǎ lì
bourbon	波本	bō běn
brandy	白兰地	bái lán dì
Budweiser	百威	bǎi wēi
Bud Ice	百威冰啤	bǎi wēi bīng pí
Canadian Club	加拿大俱乐部	jiā ná dà jù lè bù
Captain Morgan's	摩根船长	mó gēn chuán zhǎng
Carlsberg	嘉士伯	jiā shì bó
champagne	香槟酒	xiāng bīn jiǔ
Chivas Regal	芝华士	zhī huá shì
cocktail	鸡尾酒	jī wěi jiǔ
cognac	干邑白兰地	gān yì bái lán dì
Corona	科罗娜	kē luó nà
Cutty Sark	顺风威士忌	shùn fēng wēi shì jì
daiquiri	黛克瑞	dài kè ruì
draught beer	生啤，扎啤	shēng pí, zhā pí
Finlandia	芬兰伏特加	fēn lán fú tè jiā
gin	金酒	jīn jiǔ
gin and tonic	金汤力	jīn tāng lì
Gordon's	哥顿金	gē dùn jīn
Grant's	格兰金	gé lán jīn
Guinness	健力士	jiàn lì shì

Heineken	喜力	xǐ lì
J&B	珍宝	zhēn bǎo
Jack Daniels	杰克丹尼	jié kè dān ní
Jameson	占美臣	zhàn měi chén
Jim Beam	占边	zhàn biān
Johnny Walker Red	红方	hóng fāng
Johnny Walker Black	黑方	hēi fāng
Jose Cuervo	银快活	yín kuài huo
Kahlua	[甘露] 咖啡甜酒	(gān lù)kā fēi tián jiǔ
Kamikaze	日本武士	rì běn wǔ shì
Kilkenny	奇健尼	qí jiàn ní
Kirin	麒麟	qí lín
liquor/spirits	烈酒	liè jiǔ
Long Island Iced Tea	长岛冰茶	cháng dǎo bīng chá
Malibu	椰子酒	yē zi jiǎ
Manhattan	曼哈顿	màn hā dùn
Margarita	玛格丽特	mǎ gé lì tè
Martini Dry	辛辣马丁尼	xīn là mǎ dīng ní
Pabst Blue Ribbon	蓝带	lán dài
Pina Colada	椰林风光	yē lín fēng guāng
red wine	红（葡萄）酒	hóng (pú tao) jiǔ
Remy Martin	人头马	rén tóu mǎ
rum	朗姆酒	lǎng mǔ jiǔ
Rum and Coke	朗姆酒加可乐	lǎng mǔ jiā kě lè
scotch	苏格兰威士忌	sū gé lán wēi shì jì
Screwdriver	螺丝刀	sī dāo
Sex on the Beach	性感沙滩	xìng gǎn shā tān
Smirnoff	皇冠	huáng guān
Snowball	雪球	xuě qiú
Steinlager	世好	shì hǎo
Stolichnaya	苏联红牌	sū lián hóng pái
Suntory	三得利	sān dé lì
tequila	特基拉	tè jī lā
Tequila Sunrise	日升龙舌兰	rì shēng lóng shé lán

Tiger Beer	虎牌	hǔ pái
Tsingtao	青岛	qīng dǎo
vodka	伏特加	fú tè jiā
Vodka Red Bull	伏特加红牛	fú tè jiā jiā hóng niú
whiskey	威士忌	wēi shì jì
Whiskey Sour	威士忌酸	wēi shì jì suān
white wine	白葡萄酒	bái pútao jiǔ
wine	葡萄酒	pútao jiǔ

(*Published with permission from and thanks to John Pasden who compiled and first published this list at his website: sinosplice.com).

Chapter 8: Laowai Health

健康	jiànkāng	health
身体检查	shēntī jiǎnchá	medical exam
病	bìng	sick
感冒	gǎnmào	cold
流感	liúgǎn	the flu

药方	yàofáng	pharmacy
绷带	bēngdài	bandages
创可贴	chuāngkětiē	band-aids
牛黄消炎片	Niúhuáng Xiāoyán Piàn	throat tablets
康生素	kàngshēng sù	antibiotics

医院	yīyuàn	hospital
点滴	diǎndī	IV drip
医生	yīshēng	doctor
护士	hùshi	nurse
呕吐	ǒutù	vomit
发烧	fāshāo	have a fever
喉咙痛	hóulóng tòng	sore throat
咳嗽	késòu	cough
推拿	tuīná	Tui na, acupressure pinching
霜害	shuānghài	frostbite

牙医	yáyī	dentist
补牙	bǔyá	dental filling

性传播疾病	xìng chuánbò jíbìng	STD
避孕套	bìyùn tào	condom
避孕药	bìyùn yào	oral contraceptive, the Pill
吗富隆	mǎ fù long	Marvelon, oral contraceptive
敏定偶	mǐn dìng ǒu	Minulet, oral contraceptive

Extra Useful Phrases

西药	xīyào	Western medicine
中药	zhōngyào	Chinese medicine
过敏	guòmǐn	allergy
我对 X 过敏	wǒ duì X guòmǐn.	I'm allergic to X.
药方	yàofāng	prescription
救护车	jiùhù chē	ambulance
断了	duànle	broken
痛了	tòngle	painful, hurts

Chapter 9: Becoming a Travel Junkie

放假	fàngjià	go on holidays, take a vacation
旅行	lǚxíng	travel
公共交通	gōnggòng jiāotōng	public transport

火车	**huǒchē**	**train**
火车票	huǒchē piào	train tickets
慢	màn	slow
快	kuài	express
硬座	yìngzuò	hard seat
软座	ruǎnzuò	soft seat
硬卧	yìngwò	hard sleeper
上卧	shàngwò	upper bed
中卧	zhōngwò	middle bed
下卧	xiàwò	bottom bed
软卧	ruǎnwò	soft sleeper
火车站	huǒchēzhàn	train station
南	nán	south
北	běi	north
东	dōng	east
西	xī	west
火车北站	huǒchē běizhàn	north train station

公共汽车	**gōnggòngqìchē**	**bus**
空调	kōngtiáo	air conditioning
暖气	nuǎnqì	heating
汽车站	qìchēzhàn	bus station

飞机	**fēijī**	**plane**
飞机场	fēijīchǎng	airport
航空公司	hángkōng gōngsī	airline company
飞机票	fēijī piào	plane ticket
机场大巴	jīchǎng dàbā	airport shuttle bus

地铁	dìtiě	subway
出租车	**chūzū chē**	**taxi**
表	biǎo	meter
票价	piàojià	fare
通行费	tōngxíng fèi	tolls
酒店	**jiǔdiàn**	**hotel**
宿舍	sùshè	hostel
公休日	**gōng xiū rì**	**public holidays**
劳动节	láodòng jié	Labor day
国庆节	guóqìng jié	National day
春节	chūnjié	Spring Festival
清明节	qīngmíng jié	Qing Ming Festival
端午节	duānwǔ jié	Dragon Boat Festival
粽子	zòngzi	Zongzi, Steamed rice ball
中秋节	zhōngqiū jié	Mid-Autumn Festival
圣诞节	shèngdàn jié	Christmas
旅游	**lǚyóu**	**sightseeing, tourism**
长城	chángchéng	Great Wall
北京	běijīng	Beijing
紫禁城	zǐjīnchéng	The Forbidden City
颐和园	yíhé yuán	Summer Palace
天坛	tiāntán	Temple of Heaven
上海	shànghǎi	Shanghai
东方明珠塔	dōngfāng míngzhūtǎ	Oriental Pearl Tower
黄埔江	huángpǔ jiāng	Huangpu River
外滩	wàitān	the Bund
西安	xī'ān	Xi'an
兵马俑	**bīngmǎyǒng**	Terracotta Warrior Army

长江三峡大坝	chángjiāng sānxiá dà bà	3 Gorges Dam
长江	chángjiāng	Yangtze River
长江巡航	chángjiāng xúnháng	Yangtze River Cruise
桂林	guìlín	Guilin
漓江	líjiāng	Li River
拉萨	lāsà	Lhasa
西藏	xīzàng	Tibet
布达拉宫	bùdálāgōng	Potala Palace
丽江	lìjiāngshì	Lijiang Village
玉水寨	yǔ shuǐ zhài	Jade Water Village
香港	xiānggǎng	Hong Kong
嘉峪关	jiāyùguān	Jiayuguan
敦煌	dūnhuáng	Dunhuang
吐鲁番	**tǔlǔfān**	Turfan, Turpan
天山户	tiān shān hú	Tian Shan Lake
乌鲁木齐	wūlǔmùqí	Urumqi
喀什	kāshí	Kashgar

Extra Useful Phrases

上车	shàngchē	get on (bus, train, etc)
下车	xiàchē	get off (bus, train, etc)
我要去 X.	wǒ yào qù X.	I want to go to X.
两张票[到 X]	liǎng zhāng piào (dào X)	2 tickets (to X)
几点开车?	jǐdiǎn kāi chē?	What is the departure time?
几点到?	jǐdiǎn dào?	What is the arrival time?
座[号]	zuò (hào)	seat (number)

台(号)	tái (hào)	platform (number)
门口(号)	ménkǒu (hào)	gate (number)
转左	zhuànzuǒ	Turn left
专右	zhuànyòu	Turn right
这里停一下.	zhèli tíng yī xià.	Stop here.
预定	yùdìng	reservation
房间	fángjiān	room
两个晚上	liǎngge wǎnshàng	two nights
一个星期	yīge xīngqī	one week
三个人	sānge rén	three people
空的房间	kōngde fángjiān	vacancies, rooms available

www.ingramcontent.com/pod-product-compliance
Ingram Content Group UK Ltd.
Pitfield, Milton Keynes, MK11 3LW, UK
UKHW022231230426